P9-DOF-258

10,000 Most Commonly
Misspelled Words

Published by

World Book–Childcraft International, Inc.
A subsidiary of The Scott & Fetzer Company

Chicago London Sydney Tokyo Toronto

Preface

The purpose of this book is to provide a quick reference to the preferred spelling and word division of more than 10,000 commonly used—and often misspelled—words. The list was prepared by the editors of World Book from the resources of Clarence L. Barnhart, Inc.

A

a·ban·don
a·bate
ab·bey
ab·bre·vi·ate
ab·bre·vi·a·tion
ab·di·cate
ab·do·men
ab·dom·i·nal
ab·duct
a·bet
ab·hor
a·bide
a·bil·i·ty
ab·ject
a·ble
ab·nor·mal
a·board
a·bol·ish
ab·o·li·tion
a·bom·i·na·ble
a·bor·tion
a·bound
a·bout
a·bove
a·bridge
a·bridg·ment
a·broad
a·brupt
ab·scess
ab·sence
ab·sent
ab·so·lute
ab·solve
ab·sorb·ent
ab·sorp·tion
ab·stain
ab·sti·nence
ab·stract
ab·surd
a·bun·dance
a·bun·dant
a·buse
a·bys·mal

a·byss
ac·a·dem·ic
a·cad·e·my
ac·cel·er·ate
ac·cel·er·a·tor
ac·cent
ac·cept
ac·cept·a·ble
ac·cept·ance
ac·cess
ac·ces·so·ry
ac·ci·dent
ac·ci·den·tal
ac·com·mo·date
ac·com·mo·da·tion
ac·com·pa·ny
ac·com·plish
ac·cord
ac·cord·ance
ac·cord·ing·ly
ac·count
ac·count·a·bil·i·ty
ac·cred·i·ted
ac·cu·mu·late
ac·cu·mu·la·tion
ac·cur·ate
ac·curs·ed
ac·cu·sa·tion
ac·cuse
ac·cus·tom
ache
a·chieve
a·chieve·ment
ac·id
ac·knowl·edge
ac·knowl·edg·ment
a·corn
a·cous·tic
ac·quaint
ac·quaint·ance
ac·qui·esce
ac·quire
ac·qui·si·tion
ac·quit

ac·quit·tal
a·cre
a·cre·age
ac·ro·bat
a·cross
act
ac·tion
ac·tive
ac·tiv·i·ty
ac·tor
ac·tress
ac·tu·al
a·cute
ad
a·dapt
ad·ap·ta·tion
ad·dict·ed
ad·di·tion
ad·di·tive
ad·dress
ad·e·quate
ad·here
ad·he·sive
ad·ja·cent
ad·jec·tive
ad·join
ad·journ
ad·judge
ad·just
ad·min·is·ter
ad·min·is·tra·tion
ad·min·is·tra·tor
ad·mi·ra·ble
ad·mi·ral
ad·mi·ra·tion
ad·mire
ad·mis·sion
ad·mit
ad·mon·ish
ad·mo·ni·tion
ad·o·les·cent
a·dopt
a·dop·tion
a·dore

a·dorn
ad·ren·al·in
a·dult
a·dul·te·rate
a·dul·ter·y
ad·vance
ad·van·tage
ad·van·ta·geous
ad·ven·ture
ad·ven·tur·er
ad·ven·tur·ous
ad·verb
ad·ver·sar·y
ad·verse
ad·ver·si·ty
ad·ver·tise
ad·ver·tise·ment
ad·ver·tis·ing
ad·vice
ad·vis·a·ble
ad·vise
ad·vi·so·ry
ad·vo·cate
aer·i·al
aer·o·nau·tics
aer·o·sol
aes·thet·ic
af·fair
af·fect
af·fec·ta·tion
af·fec·tion
af·fec·tion·ate
af·fi·da·vit
af·firm
af·flict
af·flic·tion
af·flu·ence
af·flu·ent
af·ford
af·front
a·fire
a·float
a·foot
a·fraid

af·ter	al·ge·bra
af·ter·noon	a·li·as
af·ter·wards	al·i·bi
a·gain	al·ien
a·gainst	al·ien·ate
a·ged	a·light
a·gen·cy	a·like
a·gen·da	a·live
a·gent	al·lay
ag·gra·vate	al·le·ga·tion
ag·gres·sion	al·lege
ag·gres·sive	al·le·giance
ag·ile	al·ler·gic
ag·i·tate	al·ler·gy
ag·i·ta·tion	al·ley
a·go	al·li·ance
ag·o·ny	al·lied
a·gree	al·li·ga·tor
a·gree·a·ble	al·lo·cate
a·gree·ment	al·low
ag·ri·cul·tur·al	al·low·ance
ag·ri·cul·ture	al·loy
a·head	all right
aid	all-star
ail	al·lure
aim	al·lu·sion
air	al·ly
air-con·di·tioned	al·ma·nac
air con·di·tion·ing	al·might·y
air·craft	al·mond
air·line	al·most
air·mail	alms
air·plane	a·lone
air·port	a·long
air·tight	a·long·side
air·y	a·loof
aisle	a·loud
a·kin	al·pha·bet
a·larm	al·read·y
al·bum	al·so
al·co·hol	al·tar
ale	al·ter
a·lert	al·ter·a·tion
al·gae	al·ter·nate

al·ter·na·tive
al·though
al·ti·tude
al·to·geth·er
a·lu·mi·num
a·lum·ni
al·ways
am·a·teur
a·maze
am·bas·sa·dor
am·ber
am·big·u·ous
am·bi·tion
am·bu·lance
am·bush
a·mend
a·mend·ment
A·mer·i·can
a·mi·a·ble
a·mid
a·miss
am·mu·ni·tion
am·nes·ty
a·mong
a·mount
am·ple
am·pli·fi·er
am·pu·tate
a·muse
a·nal·y·sis
an·a·lyze
an·ar·chy
a·nat·o·my
an·ces·tor
an·chor
an·cient
an·ec·dote
a·ne·mi·a
a·ne·mic
an·es·thet·ic
a·new
an·gel
an·ger
an·gle

an·gri·ly
an·gry
an·guish
an·i·mal
an·i·mate
an·i·mos·i·ty
an·kle
an·nals
an·nex
an·ni·hi·late
an·ni·ver·sa·ry
an·no·tate
an·nounce
an·noy
an·nu·al
an·nul
a·noint
a·non·y·mous
an·oth·er
an·swer
ant
an·tag·o·nism
an·tag·o·nist
ant·arc·tic
an·te·ced·ent
an·ten·na
an·ti·bi·ot·ic
an·ti·bod·y
an·tic·i·pate
an·ti·dote
an·ti·freeze
an·ti·his·ta·mine
an·tique
an·tiq·ui·ty
an·ti-Se·mit·ic
an·ti·sep·tic
an·vil
anx·i·e·ty
anx·ious
an·y
an·y·bod·y
an·y·how
an·y·one
an·y·place

an·y·thing
an·y·time
an·y·way
an·y·where
a·part
a·part·ment
ape
a·pol·o·gize
a·pol·o·gy
a·pos·tle
ap·pall
ap·pall·ing
ap·par·el
ap·par·ent
ap·pa·ri·tion
ap·peal
ap·pear
ap·pease
ap·pen·dix
ap·pe·tite
ap·plaud
ap·plause
ap·ple
ap·pli·ance
ap·pli·cant
ap·pli·ca·tion
ap·plied
ap·ply
ap·point
ap·point·ment
ap·praise
ap·pre·ci·ate
ap·pre·ci·a·tion
ap·pre·hend
ap·pre·hen·sion
ap·pren·tice
ap·proach
ap·pro·pri·ate
ap·pro·pri·a·tion
ap·prov·al
ap·prove
ap·prox·i·mate
a·pri·cot
a·pron

apt
ap·ti·tude
a·quar·i·um
a·quat·ic
ar·bi·trar·y
ar·bi·tra·tion
arch
ar·chae·ol·o·gy
arch·bish·op
ar·chi·tect
ar·chi·tec·ture
ar·chives
arch·way
arc·tic
ar·dent
are
ar·e·a
a·re·na
ar·gue
ar·gu·ment
ar·id
a·rise
a·ris·to·crat·ic
a·rith·me·tic
ark
arm
ar·ma·ment
arm·ful
arm·hole
ar·mi·stice
ar·mor
ar·mored
ar·my
a·ro·ma
a·round
a·rouse
ar·raign
ar·range
ar·range·ment
ar·ray
ar·rears
ar·rest
ar·riv·al
ar·rive

9

ar·ro·gant
ar·row
ar·se·nal
ar·son
art
ar·te·ri·al
ar·ter·y
art·ful
ar·thri·tis
ar·ti·cle
ar·ti·fi·cial
ar·til·ler·y
ar·ti·san
art·ist
ar·tis·tic
art·less
as·bes·tos
as·cend
as·cent
as·cer·tain
ash
a·shamed
ash·es
 ·shore
a·side
ask
a·sleep
as·par·a·gus
as·pect
as·phalt
as·phyx·i·ate
as·pi·ra·tion
as·pire
as·pir·in
ass
as·sail
as·sail·ant
as·sas·si·nate
as·sas·si·na·tion
as·sault
as·sem·ble
as·sem·bly
as·sent
as·sert

as·ser·tion
as·sess
as·sess·ment
as·set
as·sign
as·sign·ment
as·sim·i·late
as·sist
as·sist·ant
as·so·ci·ate
as·so·ci·a·tion
as·sort·ment
as·sume
as·sump·tion
as·sur·ance
as·sure
as·ter
as·ter·isk
as·ton·ish
as·ton·ish·ment
as·tound
a·stray
as·trol·o·gy
as·tro·naut
as·tro·nom·i·cal
as·tron·o·my
as·tute
a·sun·der
a·sy·lum
a·sym·met·ric
ate
ath·lete
ath·let·ic
at·las
at·mos·phere
at·om
a·tom·ic
a·tone
at·tach
at·tach·ment
at·tack
at·tain
at·tempt
at·tend

at·ten·tion
at·ten·tive
at·test
at·tic
at·tire
at·ti·tude
at·tor·ney
at·tract
at·trac·tion
at·trib·ute
at·tri·tion
auc·tion
auc·tion·eer
au·da·cious
au·di·ble
au·di·ence
au·di·o·vis·u·al
au·dit
au·di·tion
au·di·to·ri·um
aug·ment
aunt
aus·pi·ces
aus·pi·cious
aus·tere
aus·ter·i·ty
au·then·tic
au·then·tic·i·ty
au·thor
au·thor·i·tar·i·an
au·thor·i·ty
au·thor·i·za·tion
au·thor·ize
au·to·bi·og·ra·phy
au·to·crat·ic
au·to·mat·ic
au·to·ma·tion
au·to·mo·bile
au·ton·o·mous
au·top·sy
au·tumn
aux·il·ia·ry
a·vail
a·vail·a·ble

av·a·lanche
av·ar·ice
a·venge
av·e·nue
av·er·age
a·ver·sion
a·vert
av·id
a·void
a·wait
a·wake
a·wak·en
a·ward
a·ware
a·way
awe
aw·ful
a·while
awk·ward
ax
ax·is
ax·le
aye

B

bab·ble
babe
ba·by
ba·by-sit
ba·by sit·ter
bach·e·lor
back
back·ache
back·bone
back·fire
back·gam·mon
back·ground
back·hand·ed
back·ward
ba·con
bac·ter·i·a
badge
baf·fle

bag·gage
bag·pipe
bail
bait
bake
bak·er
bal·ance
bal·co·ny
bald
balk
ball
bal·lad
bal·let
bal·lis·tic
bal·loon
bal·lot
ball·point
balm
bam·boo
ba·nan·a
band
band·age
ban·dit
bang
ban·ish
ban·jo
bank
bank·er
bank·rupt
bank·rupt·cy
ban·ner
ban·quet
bap·tism
Bap·tist
bap·tize
bar
bar·bar·i·an
bar·bar·ic
bar·ba·rous
bar·be·cue
bar·ber
bard
bare
bare·foot

bar·gain
barge
bark
bar·ley
barn
barn·yard
ba·rom·e·ter
bar·o·met·ric
bar·racks
bar·rel
bar·ren
bar·ri·cade
bar·ri·er
bar·ter
base
base·ball
base·ment
bash·ful
ba·sic
ba·sin
ba·sis
bask
bas·ket
bas·ket·ball
bas·tard
baste
batch
bath
bathe
bath·robe
bath·room
ba·ton
bat·tal·ion
bat·ter·y
bat·tle
bat·tle·field
bat·tle·ment
bat·tle·ship
bau·ble
bawl
bay
bay·o·net
ba·zaar
beach

bea·con
bead
beak
beam
bean
bear
bear·a·ble
beard
bear·er
bear·ing
beast
beat
beat·en
beau·ti·fi·ca·tion
beau·ti·ful
beau·ti·fy
beau·ty
bea·ver
be·came
be·cause
beck
beck·on
be·come
be·com·ing
bed·ding
bed·lam
bed·room
bed·spread
bed·stead
bed·time
bee
beech
beef
bee·hive
been
beer
beet
bee·tle
be·fore
be·fore·hand
be·friend
be·fud·dle
be·gan
be·get

beg·gar
be·gin
be·gin·ner
be·gin·ning
be·gone
be·got
be·gun
be·half
be·have
be·hav·ior
be·head
be·held
be·hind
be·hold
be·ing
be·lat·ed
belch
bel·fry
be·lie
be·lief
be·lieve
be·liev·er
be·lit·tle
bell
belle
bel·lig·er·ent
bel·low
bel·ly
be·long
be·lov·ed
be·low
belt
be·moan
bench
bend
be·neath
ben·e·dic·tion
ben·e·fac·tor
ben·e·fi·cial
ben·e·fi·ci·ar·y
ben·e·fit
be·nev·o·lence
be·nev·o·lent
be·nign

bent
be·queath
be·quest
be·reave
be·reft
be·ret
ber·ry
be·set
be·side
be·sides
be·siege
best
be·stow
be·tray
be·tray·al
be·trothed
bet·ter
be·tween
bev·er·age
be·wail
be·ware
be·wil·der
be·witch
be·yond
bi·an·nu·al
bi·as
Bi·ble
bib·li·cal
bib·li·og·ra·phy
bick·er
bi·cy·cle
bid·der
bide
bi·en·ni·al
bier
big·ger
big·gest
bilge
bill
bil·liards
bil·lion
bil·low
bi·na·ry
bind

bind·er
bin·go
bi·noc·u·lars
bi·o·chem·is·try
bi·og·ra·phy
bi·o·log·i·cal
bi·ol·o·gy
birch
bird
bird·house
bird·ie
bird's-eye
birth
birth·day
birth·place
birth rate
birth·right
bis·cuit
bish·op
bi·son
bite
bit·ter
bi·zarre
black
black·ber·ry
black·bird
black·board
black·en
black eye
black·list
black·mail
black mar·ket
black·out
black·smith
blad·der
blade
blame
blanch
bland
blank
blan·ket
blas·phe·my
blast
bla·tant

blaze
bleach
bleak
bleat
bled
bleed
blem·ish
blend
bless
bless·ed
bless·ing
blew
blight
blind
blink
bliss
bliss·ful
blis·ter
blithe
bliz·zard
bloat
blond
blood
blood pres·sure
blood·stream
blood·y
bloom
blos·som
blot
blotch
blouse
blow
blow·out
blow·torch
blub·ber
blue
blue·ber·ry
blue·bird
blue·grass
blue jay
blue·print
bluff
blun·der
blunt

blur
blush
blus·ter
boar
board
board·er
boast
boat
bode
bod·y
bod·y·guard
bog·gle
boil
boil·er
bois·ter·ous
bold
bo·lo·gna
bol·ster
bolt
bomb
bom·bard
bomb·shell
bond
bond·age
bonds·man
bone
bon·fire
bon·net
bo·nus
book
book·case
book·keep·er
book·keep·ing
book·let
book·sell·er
book·shelf
book·shop
book·store
boom
boon
boost
boot
booth
boo·ty

bo·rax	branch
bor·der	brand
bore	bran·dish
bore·dom	brand-new
bor·ough	bran·dy
bor·row	brass
bos·om	brave
boss	brav·er·y
boss·y	brawl
bo·tan·i·cal	brawn
bot·a·ny	bra·zen
both	breach
both·er	bread
bot·tle	breadth
bot·tom	break
bough	break·a·ble
bought	break·down
bouil·lon	break·er
boul·der	break·fast
bounce	break·through
bound	breast
bound·ar·y	breath
boun·ti·ful	breathe
boun·ty	breath·less
bou·quet	bred
bour·bon	breech
bout	breech·es
bow	breed
bow·el	breed·ing
bowl	breeze
bowl·ing	breez·y
box	brev·i·ty
box·er	brew
boy	bribe
boy·cott	brib·er·y
boy·hood	brick
brace	brid·al
brace·let	bride
brack·et	bridge
brag	bri·dle
braid	brief
brain	bri·gade
brake	brig·a·dier
bran	bright

bright·en	buck
bril·liance	buck·et
bril·liant	buck·le
brim	buck·shot
brine	buck·skin
bring	buck·wheat
brink	budge
brisk	budg·et
bris·tle	buff
Brit·ain	buf·fa·lo
Brit·ish	buff·er
brit·tle	buf·fet
broad	bug·gy
broad·cast	build
broad·cloth	build·er
broad·en	build·ing
broad·loom	build-up
broad-mind·ed	built
broad·side	built-in
broc·co·li	bulb
broil	bulge
broil·er	bulk
broke	bull
bro·ken	bull·dog
bro·ker	bull·doz·er
bronze	bul·let
brooch	bul·le·tin
brood	bull·fight·er
brook	bul·lion
broom	bul·ly
broth	bul·wark
broth·er	bump
broth·er·hood	bump·er
brought	bump·y
brow	bunch
brown	bun·dle
brown·ie	bun·gle
browse	bun·ion
bruise	bun·ny
brush	bun·ting
bru·tal	buoy
brute	buoy·ant
brut·ish	bur·den
bub·ble	bur·eau

bu·reauc·ra·cy
bur·glar
bur·i·al
bur·ied
bur·lap
bur·lesque
burn
burn·er
bur·nish
burr
burst
bur·y
bush
bush·el
bush·y
bus·i·ly
busi·ness
bust
bus·tle
bus·y
butch·er
butt
but·ter
but·ter·fly
but·ter·milk
but·ton
but·ton·hole
but·tress
buy
buy·er
buzz
by-pass
by-prod·uct
by·stand·er

C

cab·bage
cab·driv·er
cab·in
cab·i·net
ca·ble
cack·le
ca·fe

caf·e·te·ri·a
caf·feine
cage
cake
ca·lam·i·ty
cal·cu·late
cal·cu·la·tion
cal·cu·la·tor
cal·en·dar
calf
cal·i·ber
cal·i·co
call
call·er
cal·lous
calm
cal·o·rie
calves
came
cam·el
cam·er·a
cam·er·a·man
cam·ou·flage
camp
cam·paign
camp·er
ca·nal
ca·nar·y
can·cel
can·cel·la·tion
can·cer
can·cer·ous
can·did
can·di·da·cy
can·di·date
can·dle
can·dle·stick
can·dor
can·dy
cane
ca·nine
can·ker
canned
can·ni·bal

can·non
ca·noe
can·o·py
can't
can·yon
ca·pa·bil·i·ty
ca·pa·ble
ca·pac·i·ty
cape
ca·per
cap·i·tal
cap·i·tal·ism
cap·i·tal·ize
ca·pit·u·late
ca·price
ca·pri·cious
cap·size
cap·sule
cap·tain
cap·tion
cap·ti·vate
cap·tive
cap·tiv·i·ty
cap·ture
car
car·a·mel
car·at
car·a·van
car·bo·hy·drate
car·bon
car·bun·cle
car·bu·re·tor
car·cass
card
card·board
car·di·gan
car·di·nal
care
ca·reer
care·ful
care·less
ca·ress
car·go
car·i·ca·ture

car·ies
car·nal
car·ni·val
car·niv·o·rous
car·ol
ca·rouse
car·pen·ter
car·pet
car·riage
car·ri·er
car·rot
car·ry
cart
car·tel
cart·er
car·ti·lage
car·tog·ra·phy
car·ton
car·toon
car·tridge
carve
case
cash
cash·ier
cash·mere
cas·ing
ca·si·no
cas·ket
cas·se·role
cast
cast·er
cast·ing
cas·tle
cas·tor
cas·u·al
cas·u·al·ty
cat·a·log
cat·a·lyst
cat·a·ract
ca·tas·tro·phe
catch
cat·e·chism
cat·e·gor·i·cal
cat·e·go·ry

ca·ter
cat·er·pil·lar
ca·the·dral
Cath·o·lic
cat·nip
cat·tle
cat·ty
caught
cau·li·flow·er
caulk
cause
caus·tic
cau·ter·ize
cau·tion
cau·tious
cav·a·lier
cav·al·ry
cave
cave-in
cav·ern
cease
cease·less
ce·dar
cede
ceil·ing
cel·e·brate
cel·e·bra·tion
ce·leb·ri·ty
cel·er·y
ce·les·tial
cell
cel·lar
cel·lo·phane
cel·lu·lar
cel·lu·lose
Cel·si·us
ce·ment
cem·e·ter·y
cen·sor
cen·sor·ship
cen·sure
cen·sus
cent
cen·ter

cen·ti·grade
cen·ti·me·ter
cen·ti·pede
cen·tral
cen·tral·i·za·tion
cen·tral·ize
cen·tur·y
ce·ram·ic
cer·e·al
ce·re·bral
cer·e·mo·ni·al
cer·e·mo·ny
cer·tain
cer·tain·ty
cer·tif·i·cate
cer·ti·fi·ca·tion
cer·ti·fied
cer·ti·fy
ces·sa·tion
chafe
chaff
chain
chair
chair·man
chair·per·son
chalk
chalk·board
chal·lenge
cham·ber
cham·ber·maid
cham·pagne
cham·pi·on
chance
chan·cel·lor
chan·de·lier
change
change·a·ble
chan·nel
chant
cha·os
cha·ot·ic
chap·el
chap·lain
chap·ter

char·ac·ter
char·ac·ter·is·tic
char·ac·ter·ize
cha·rade
char·coal
charge
charge·a·ble
cha·ris·ma
char·i·ta·ble
char·i·ty
charm
chart
char·ter
chase
chas·sis
chaste
chas·tise
chas·ti·ty
chat
chat·tel
chat·ter
chauf·feur
chau·vin·ism
cheap
cheat
check
check·book
check·ered
check·er
check·list
check·mate
check·point
check·up
cheek
cheer
cheer·ful
cheer·i·ness
cheer·y
cheese
chef
chem·i·cal
chem·is·try
cher·ish
cher·ry

chess
chest
chest·nut
chew
chew·y
chick
chick·en
chide
chief
chif·fon
child
child·birth
child·hood
child·ish
child·like
chil·dren
chill
chill·y
chime
chim·ney
chim·pan·zee
chin
chi·na
Chi·nese
chink
chip
chi·ro·prac·tor
chirp
chis·el
chiv·al·rous
chiv·al·ry
chlo·ride
chlo·rine
chlo·ro·phyll
choc·o·late
choice
choir
choke
cho·les·ter·ol
choose
chop
chop·per
cho·ral
chord

cho·re·og·ra·pher
cho·rus
chose
cho·sen
Christ
chris·ten
Chris·tian
Chris·ti·an·i·ty
Christ·mas
chro·mi·um
chro·mo·some
chron·ic
chron·i·cle
chron·o·log·i·cal
chry·san·the·mum
chuck
chuck·le
chum
church
church·go·er
church·yard
churn
chute
ci·der
ci·gar
cig·a·rette
cinch
cin·der
cin·e·ma
cin·na·mon
ci·pher
cir·cle
cir·cuit
cir·cu·lar
cir·cu·late
cir·cu·la·tion
cir·cu·la·to·ry
cir·cum·fer·ence
cir·cum·scribe
cir·cum·stance
cir·cum·stan·tial
cir·cus
ci·ta·tion
cite

cit·i·zen
cit·ric
cit·rus
cit·y
civ·ic
civ·il
ci·vil·ian
ci·vil·i·ty
civ·i·li·za·tion
civ·i·lize
clad
claim
clam
clam·mi·ness
clam·my
clam·or
clamp
clan
clan·des·tine
clang
clank
clap
clap·board
clar·i·fy
clar·i·ty
clash
clasp
class
clas·sic
clas·si·cal
clas·si·fi·ca·tion
clas·si·fied
clas·si·fy
class·mate
class·room
clat·ter
clause
claw
clay
clean
clean·er
cleanse
cleans·er
clear

clear·ance
cleav·age
cleave
clef
cleft
clem·en·cy
clench
cler·gy
cler·gy·man
clerk
clev·er
cli·ent
cli·en·tele
cliff
cli·mate
cli·mat·ic
cli·max
climb
clinch
cling
clin·i·cal
clink
clip
clip·board
clip·pers
clique
cloak
clock
clock·wise
clock·work
clod
clog
clois·ter
close
clos·et
cloth
clothe
clóthes
cloth·ing
cloud
cloud·i·ness
cloud·y
clout
clove

clo·ver
clown
club
cluck
clue
clump
clum·si·ness
clum·sy
clung
clus·ter
clutch
clut·ter
coach
co·ag·u·late
co·a·li·tion
coarse
coast
coat
coax
co·balt
cob·bler
co·bra
cob·web
co·caine
cock
cock·pit
cock·tail
cock·y
co·coa
co·co·nut
co·coon
code
co·ed
co·ef·fi·cient
co·er·cion
co·ex·ist·ence
cof·fee
cof·fee·pot
cof·fin
co·gent
co·gnac
co·her·ence
co·her·ent
co·he·sive

coil
coin
co·in·cide
co·in·ci·dence
co·in·ci·den·tal
coke
cold
cole·slaw
col·ic
col·lab·o·rate
col·lage
col·lapse
col·laps·i·ble
col·lar
col·lat·er·al
col·lect
col·lec·tion
col·lec·tive
col·lec·tor
col·lege
col·lide
col·lie
col·li·sion
co·logne
co·lon
colo·nel
co·lo·ni·al
col·o·nist
col·o·ni·za·tion
col·o·nize
col·o·ny
col·or
co·los·sal
colt
col·umn
co·ma
comb
com·bat
com·bi·na·tion
com·bine
com·bus·ti·ble
com·bus·tion
come
co·me·di·an

com·e·dy
com·et
com·fort
com·fort·a·ble
com·fort·er
com·ic
com·ing
com·ma
com·mand
com·mand·er
com·mand·ment
com·mem·o·rate
com·mence
com·mend
com·men·sur·ate
com·ment
com·men·tar·y
com·men·ta·tor
com·merce
com·mer·cial
com·mis·sion
com·mis·sion·er
com·mit
com·mit·tee
com·mod·i·ty
com·mon
com·mon·place
com·mon·wealth
com·mo·tion
com·mu·nal
com·mune
com·mu·ni·cate
com·mu·ni·ca·tion
com·mun·ion
com·mu·nism
com·mu·ni·ty
com·mute
com·mut·er
com·pact
com·pan·ion
com·pa·ny
com·par·a·ble
com·par·a·tive
com·pare

com·par·i·son
com·part·ment
com·pass
com·pas·sion
com·pat·i·ble
com·pel
com·pen·sate
com·pen·sa·tion
com·pete
com·pe·tence
com·pe·tent
com·pe·ti·tion
com·pet·i·tive
com·pet·i·tor
com·pile
com·plain
com·plaint
com·ple·ment
com·plete
com·ple·tion
com·plex
com·plex·ion
com·pli·ance
com·pli·cate
com·pli·cat·ed
com·pli·ca·tion
com·pli·ment
com·pli·men·ta·ry
com·ply
com·po·nent
com·pose
com·pos·ite
com·po·si·tion
com·po·sure
com·pound
com·pre·hen·sion
com·pre·hen·sive
com·press
com·prise
com·pro·mise
comp·trol·ler
com·pul·sion
com·pul·so·ry
com·put·er

con·ceal
con·cede
con·ceit
con·ceiv·a·ble
con·ceive
con·cen·trate
con·cen·tra·tion
con·cept
con·cep·tion
con·cern
con·cerned
con·cern·ing
con·cert
con·ces·sion
con·cil·i·a·to·ry
con·cise
con·clude
con·clu·sion
con·cord
con·crete
con·cur
con·cur·rent
con·demn
con·dem·na·tion
con·den·sa·tion
con·dense
con·de·scend
con·di·tion
con·du·cive
con·duct
con·duc·tor
cone
con·fed·er·a·cy
con·fed·er·ate
con·fed·e·ra·tion
con·fer
con·fer·ence
con·fess
con·fes·sion
con·fide
con·fi·dence
con·fi·dent
con·fi·den·tial
con·fig·u·ra·tion

con·fine
con·firm
con·fir·ma·tion
con·fis·cate
con·flict
con·form
con·form·i·ty
con·found
con·front
con·fuse
con·fu·sion
con·gen·ial
con·gen·i·tal
con·ges·tion
con·grat·u·late
con·grat·u·la·tion
con·gre·gate
con·gre·ga·tion
con·gress
con·gres·sion·al
con·jec·ture
con·junc·tion
con·nect
con·nec·tion
con·quer
con·quer·or
con·quest
con·science
con·sci·en·tious
con·scious
con·se·crate
con·sec·u·tive
con·sen·sus
con·sent
con·se·quence
con·se·quent·ly
con·ser·va·tion
con·serv·a·tive
con·serv·a·to·ry
con·serve
con·sid·er
con·sid·er·a·ble
con·sid·er·a·tion
con·sign·ment

con·sist
con·sist·ent
con·sole
con·sol·i·date
con·so·nant
con·spic·u·ous
con·spir·a·cy
con·spire
con·stant
con·stel·la·tion
con·sti·pa·tion
con·stit·u·ent
con·sti·tute
con·sti·tu·tion
con·strain
con·straint
con·strict
con·struct
con·struc·tion
con·sul
con·su·late
con·sult
con·sul·ta·tion
con·sume
con·sum·er
con·sump·tion
con·tact
con·ta·gion
con·ta·gious
con·tain
con·tain·er
con·tam·i·nate
con·tam·i·na·tion
con·tem·plate
con·tem·pla·tion
con·tem·po·rar·y
con·tempt
con·tempt·i·ble
con·temp·tu·ous
con·tend
con·tent
con·ten·tion
con·test
con·test·ant

con·ti·nent	co·op·e·ra·tion
con·ti·nen·tal	co·op·e·ra·tive
con·tin·gent	co·or·di·nate
con·tin·u·al	co·or·di·na·tion
con·tin·u·a·tion	cope
con·tin·ue	cop·ing
con·tin·u·ous	cop·per
con·tract	cop·y
con·trac·tion	cop·y·right
con·trac·tor	cor·al
con·tra·dict	cord
con·tra·dic·tion	cor·dial
con·tra·ry	cor·du·roy
con·trast	core
con·trib·ute	cork
con·tri·bu·tion	corn
con·trive	cor·ne·a
con·trol	cor·ner
con·trol·ler	cor·ner·stone
con·tro·ver·sial	cor·nice
con·tro·ver·sy	corn·stalk
con·va·les·cence	cor·ol·lar·y
con·vene	cor·o·nar·y
con·ven·ience	cor·o·na·tion
con·ven·ient	cor·o·ner
con·vent	cor·po·ral
con·ven·tion	cor·por·ate
con·verge	cor·po·ra·tion
con·ver·sa·tion	corps
con·verse	corpse
con·ver·sion	cor·ral
con·vert	cor·rect
con·vey	cor·rec·tion
con·vey·or	cor·re·late
con·vict	cor·res·pond
con·vic·tion	cor·res·pond·ence
con·vince	cor·res·pond·ent
con·vul·sion	cor·ri·dor
cook	cor·rode
cook·ie	cor·ro·sion
cook·out	cor·ru·gat·ed
cool	cor·rupt
cool·er	cor·rup·tion
co·op·e·rate	cor·ti·sone

27

cos·met·ic
cos·mic
cost
cost·ly
cos·tume
cot·tage
cot·ton
couch
cough
could
coun·cil
coun·ci·lor
coun·sel
coun·se·lor
count
count·down
coun·te·nance
count·er
coun·ter·act
coun·ter·feit
coun·ter·part
coun·ter·sign
count·ess
count·less
coun·try
coun·try·man
coun·try·side
coun·ty
coup
cou·ple
cou·pon
cour·age
cou·ra·geous
cour·i·er
course
court
cour·te·ous
cour·te·sy
court·house
court-mar·tial
court·room
court·yard
cous·in
cove

cov·e·nant
cov·er
cov·er·age
cov·ert
cov·et·ous
cow·ard
cow·hide
coy
coy·ote
co·zy
crab
crack
crack·er
crack·le
cra·dle
craft
crafts·man
craft·y
crag
cram
cramp
cran·ber·ry
crane
crank
crash
crate
cra·ter
crave
crawl
cray·on
craze
cra·zy
creak
cream
cream·er·y
cream·y
crease
cre·ate
cre·a·tion
cre·a·tive
cre·a·tor
crea·ture
cre·den·tials
cred·it

cred·i·tor
cred·u·lous
creed
creek
creep
cre·mate
crepe
crept
cre·scen·do
cres·cent
crest
crev·ice
crew
crib
crick·et
cried
cries
crime
crim·i·nal
crimp
crim·son
cringe
crin·kle
crip·ple
cri·sis
crisp
criss·cross
cri·te·ri·on
crit·ic
crit·i·cal
crit·i·cism
crit·i·cize
croak
cro·chet
croc·o·dile
crook
crop
cross
cross·breed
cross-ex·am·ine
cross-eyed
cross-pur·pose
cross-ref·er·ence
cross·road

cross-sec·tion
cross·walk
cross·word
crotch
crouch
crow
crowd
crown
cru·cial
cru·ci·fy
crude
cruel
cru·el·ty
cruise
crumb
crum·ble
cru·sade
crush
crust
crutch
cry
crys·tal
crys·tal·lize
cube
cu·bic
cuck·oo
cu·cum·ber
cud·dle
cue
cuff
cul·sine
cu·li·nar·y
cul·mi·nate
cul·pa·ble
cul·prit
cult
cul·ti·vate
cul·ti·va·tion
cul·ti·va·tor
cul·tur·al
cul·ture
cum·ber·some
cu·mu·la·tive
cun·ning

cup·cake
cup·ful
cur·a·ble
cu·ra·tor
curb
cure
cur·few
cur·i·os·i·ty
cur·i·ous
curl
curl·y
cur·ren·cy
cur·rent
cur·ric·u·lum
curse
cur·sor·y
cur·tail
cur·tain
curve
cush·ion
cus·tard
cus·to·di·an
cus·to·dy
cus·tom
cus·tom·ar·y
cus·tom·er
cut·back
cute
cut·ler·y
cut·let
cut·off
cut·out
cut·ter
cy·cle
cy·clic
cy·clone
cyl·in·der
cym·bal
cyn·i·cal
cy·press

D

dab·ble

Da·cron
dag·ger
dai·ly
dain·ty
dair·y
dai·sy
dam·age
dame
damn
dam·na·tion
damp
damp·er
dance
danc·er
dan·de·li·on
dan·druff
dan·dy
dan·ger
dan·ger·ous
dan·gle
Dan·ish
dare
dar·ing
dark
dark·en
dar·ling
darn
dart
dash
da·ta
date
daub
daugh·ter
dawn
day
day·break
day·dream
day·light
day·time
daze
daz·zle
dea·con
dead
dead·en

dead·line
dead·lock
dead·ly
deaf
deaf·en
deal
deal·er
deal·ing
dean
dear
death
death·bed
de·ba·cle
de·base
de·bat·a·ble
de·bate
deb·it
de·bris
debt
debt·or
de·but
dec·ade
de·ca·dent
de·cal
de·cay
de·cease
de·ceit
de·ceive
de·cen·cy
de·cent
de·cep·tion
de·cide
de·cid·ed·ly
dec·i·mal
de·ci·sion
de·ci·sive
deck
dec·la·ra·tion
de·clare
de·cline
de·code
de·com·pose
de·com·pres·sion
dec·o·rate

dec·o·ra·tion
de·coy
de·crease
de·cree
ded·i·cate
ded·i·ca·tion
de·duct
de·duc·tion
deed
deem
deep
deep·en
deer
de·face
de·fault
de·feat
de·fect
de·fec·tive
de·fend
de·fend·ant
de·fense
de·fen·sive
de·fer
def·er·ence
de·fi·ance
de·fi·ant
de·fi·cien·cy
def·i·cit
de·file
de·fine
def·i·nite
def·i·ni·tion
de·fin·i·tive
de·form
de·formed
de·form·i·ty
de·fraud
de·funct
de·fy
de·gen·e·rate
deg·ra·da·tion
de·grade
de·gree
de·hy·drate

deign
de·i·ty
de·ject·ed
de·lay
del·e·gate
del·e·ga·tion
de·lib·er·ate
de·lib·e·ra·tion
del·i·ca·cy
del·i·cate
del·i·ca·tes·sen
de·li·cious
de·light
de·light·ful
de·lin·quent
de·lir·i·ous
de·liv·er
de·liv·er·y
del·ta
de·lude
de·lu·sion
de·mand
de·mean·or
de·ment·ed
de·moc·ra·cy
dem·o·crat
dem·o·crat·ic
de·mol·ish
dem·o·li·tion
de·mon
dem·on·strate
dem·on·stra·tion
dem·on·stra·tive
dem·on·stra·tor
de·mor·al·ize
de·mo·tion
de·ni·al
den·im
de·nom·i·na·tion
de·note
de·nounce
dense
den·si·ty
den·tal

den·tist
de·nun·ci·a·tion
de·ny
de·o·dor·ant
de·part
de·part·ment
de·par·ture
de·pend
de·pend·a·ble
de·pend·ence
de·pend·en·cy
de·pend·ent
de·plore
de·por·ta·tion
de·pose
de·pos·it
dep·o·si·tion
de·pot
de·pre·ci·a·tion
de·press
de·pres·sant
de·pres·sion
de·prive
depth
dep·u·ty
de·ranged
de·ride
de·ri·sion
der·i·va·tion
de·rive
de·rog·a·to·ry
de·scend
de·scend·ant
de·scent
de·scribe
de·scrip·tion
de·seg·re·gate
de·seg·re·ga·tion
des·ert
de·serve
de·sign
des·ig·nate
des·ig·na·tion
de·sir·a·ble

de·sire
desk
des·o·late
des·o·la·tion
de·spair
des·per·ate
des·per·a·tion
de·spise
de·spite
de·spond·ent
des·sert
des·ti·na·tion
des·tine
des·ti·ny
des·ti·tute
de·stroy
de·struc·tion
de·struc·tive
de·tach
de·tail
de·tain
de·tect
de·tec·tive
de·tec·tor
de·ten·tion
de·ter·gent
de·ter·i·o·rate
de·ter·mi·na·tion
de·ter·mine
de·ter·rent
de·test
de·test·a·ble
de·tour
de·tract
det·ri·men·tal
de·val·u·a·tion
de·val·ue
dev·as·tate
dev·as·ta·tion
de·vel·op
de·vel·op·ment
de·vi·a·tion
de·vice
dev·il

de·vi·ous
de·vise
de·vote
de·vo·tion
de·vour
de·vout
dew
dex·ter·i·ty
di·a·be·tes
di·ag·nose
di·ag·no·sis
di·ag·nos·tic
di·ag·o·nal
di·a·gram
di·al
di·a·lect
di·a·logue
di·am·e·ter
dia·mond
di·a·per
di·a·phragm
di·ar·rhe·a
di·a·ry
dice
dic·tate
dic·ta·tion
dic·ta·tor
dic·ta·to·ri·al
dic·tion·ar·y
die
die·sel
di·et
di·e·tet·ic
dif·fer
dif·fer·ence
dif·fer·ent
dif·fe·ren·tial
dif·fi·cult
dif·fi·cul·ty
dif·fuse
dif·fu·sion
di·gest
di·ges·tion
dig·ger

dig·it·al
dig·ni·fied
dig·ni·fy
dig·ni·tar·y
dig·ni·ty
di·gress
di·gres·sion
di·late
di·la·tion
di·lem·ma
dil·i·gence
dil·i·gent
di·lute
di·lu·tion
dime
di·men·sion
di·min·ish
di·min·u·tive
dim·ple
dine
din·er
din·ner
di·no·saur
di·o·cese
di·plo·ma
di·plo·ma·cy
dip·lo·mat
dire
di·rect
di·rec·tion
di·rec·tor
di·rec·to·ry
dirt
dirt·y
dis·a·bil·i·ty
dis·ad·van·tage
dis·a·gree
dis·a·gree·a·ble
dis·ap·pear
dis·ap·pear·ance
dis·ap·point
dis·ap·point·ment
dis·ap·prov·al
dis·ap·prove

dis·arm
dis·ar·ma·ment
dis·ar·ray
dis·as·ter
dis·as·trous
dis·burse·ment
disc
dis·card
dis·cern
dis·charge
dis·ci·pline
dis·claim
dis·close
dis·clo·sure
dis·com·fit
dis·com·fort
dis·con·nect
dis·con·tent·ed
dis·con·tin·ue
dis·cord
dis·cord·ant
dis·count
dis·cour·age
dis·course
dis·cour·te·ous
dis·cov·er
dis·cov·er·y
dis·cred·it
dis·creet
dis·cre·tion
dis·crim·i·nate
dis·crim·i·na·tion
dis·cuss
dis·cus·sion
dis·dain
dis·ease
dis·en·chant·ment
dis·en·gage
dis·fav·or
dis·fig·ure
dis·grace
dis·grace·ful
dis·guise
dis·gust

dish
di·shev·eled
dis·hon·est
dis·hon·or
dis·il·lu·sion
dis·in·fect
dis·in·fect·ant
dis·in·her·it
dis·in·te·grate
dis·in·te·gra·tion
dis·in·ter·est·ed
dis·joint·ed
disk
dis·like
dis·lo·cate
dis·mal
dis·man·tle
dis·may
dis·miss
dis·miss·al
dis·mount
dis·o·be·di·ence
dis·o·be·di·ent
dis·o·bey
dis·or·der
dis·or·der·ly
dis·or·gan·ize
dis·own
dis·patch·er
dis·pel
dis·pen·sa·tion
dis·pense
dis·perse
dis·place
dis·play
dis·please
dis·pleas·ure
dis·pos·al
dis·pose
dis·po·si·tion
dis·pro·por·tion·ate
dis·pute
dis·qual·i·fy
dis·qui·et

dis·re·gard
dis·rep·u·ta·ble
dis·re·spect
dis·rup·tion
dis·sat·is·fac·tion
dis·sat·is·fied
dis·sect
dis·sem·i·nate
dis·sen·sion
dis·sent
dis·ser·ta·tion
dis·serv·ice
dis·sim·i·lar
dis·si·pate
dis·so·lu·tion
dis·solve
dis·suade
dis·tance
dis·tant
dis·taste·ful
dis·till
dis·till·er·y
dis·tinct
dis·tinc·tion
dis·tin·guish
dis·tort
dis·tract
dis·trac·tion
dis·tress
dis·trib·ute
dis·tri·bu·tion
dis·trib·u·tor
dis·trict
dis·trust
dis·turb
dis·turb·ance
ditch
dive
di·verge
di·ver·gent
di·verse
di·ver·si·fy
di·ver·sion
di·ver·si·ty

di·vert
di·vide
div·i·dend
di·vid·er
di·vine
di·vin·i·ty
di·vi·sion
di·vi·sor
di·vorce
di·vulge
diz·zy
doc·ile
dock
doc·tor
doc·trine
doc·u·ment
doc·u·men·tar·y
dodge
do·er
does
dog·house
dog·ma
dog·mat·ic
doi·ly
doll
dol·lar
doll·house
doll·y
dol·phin
do·main
dome
do·mes·tic
dom·i·nant
dom·i·nate
dom·i·na·tion
dom·i·neer·ing
do·min·ion
dom·i·no
do·na·tion
done
don·key
do·nor
doom
door

door·bell
door·knob
door·man
door·step
door·way
dor·mant
dor·mi·to·ry
dose
dou·ble
dou·bly
doubt
doubt·ful
dough
dough·nut
dove
down
down·cast
down·fall
down·hill
down·pour
down·right
down·stairs
down·town
down·ward
down·y
doze
doz·en
drab
draft
drag
drain
drain·age
dra·ma
dra·mat·ic
dram·a·tize
drank
drape
dra·per·y
dras·tic
draw
draw·back
drawer
drawl
drawn

dread·ful
dream
drear·y
dredge
drench
dress
dress·er
dress·mak·er
drew
drib·ble
dried
drift
drift·wood
drill
drink
drip
drive
drive-in
driv·er
drive·way
driz·zle
drool
droop
drop
drop-out
drought
drove
drown
drow·si·ness
drow·sy
drudge
drudg·er·y
drug
drug·gist
drug·store
drum
drunk
drunk·ard
drunk·en
dry
dry-clean
dry clean·ing
dry·er
du·al

duch·ess
duck
duct
dude
due
du·el
du·et
dug·out
duke
dull
dumb
dumb·bell
dumb·wait·er
dum·found
dump
dunce
dun·ga·rees
dun·geon
du·plex
du·pli·cate
du·plic·i·ty
du·ra·ble
du·ra·tion
dur·ing
dusk
dusk·y
dust
dust·er
dust·y
du·ti·a·ble
du·ty
dwarf
dwell
dwell·ing
dwin·dle
dye
dye·ing
dy·ing
dy·nam·ic
dy·na·mite

E

each

ea·ger
ea·gle
ear
ear·ly
ear·mark
earn
ear·nest
earn·ings
earth
earth·en·ware
earth·ly
earth·quake
ease
eas·i·ly
east
east·ern
east·ward
eas·y
eat
eaves
ebb
eb·on·y
ec·cen·tric
ec·cle·si·as·ti·cal
ech·o
e·clipse
e·col·o·gy
e·co·nom·ic
e·co·nom·i·cal
e·con·o·mist
e·con·o·mize
e·con·o·my
ec·sta·sy
edge
edg·ing
ed·i·ble
e·di·tion
ed·i·tor
ed·u·cate
ed·u·ca·tion
ed·u·ca·tion·al
eel
ef·fect
ef·fec·tive

ef·fec·tu·al
ef·fer·ves·cent
ef·fi·cien·cy
ef·fi·cient
ef·fort
egg
egg·shell
e·go·tism
eight
eight·een
eight·eenth
eighth
eight·i·eth
eight·y
ei·ther
e·ject
e·jec·tion
e·lab·or·ate
e·lapse
e·las·tic
e·late
el·bow
eld·er
e·lect
e·lec·tion
e·lec·tive
e·lec·tor
e·lec·tric
e·lec·tri·cal
e·lec·tri·cian
e·lec·tric·i·ty
e·lec·tri·fy
e·lec·tron
e·lec·tron·ic
e·lec·tron·i·cal·ly
e·lec·tron·ics
el·e·gance
el·e·gant
el·e·ment
el·e·men·tar·y
el·e·phant
el·e·vate
el·e·va·tion
el·e·va·tor

e·lev·en
e·lev·enth
el·i·gi·ble
e·lim·i·nate
e·lite
elm
el·o·quence
el·o·quent
else
else·where
e·lude
e·lu·sive
e·man·ci·pa·tion
em·bar·go
em·bark
em·bar·rass
em·bas·sy
em·bat·tled
em·bel·lish
em·ber
em·blem
em·bod·y
em·boss
em·brace
em·broi·der
em·broi·der·y
em·bry·o
em·er·ald
e·merge
e·mer·gen·cy
em·i·grant
em·i·grate
em·i·gra·tion
em·i·nence
em·i·nent
e·mis·sion
e·mit
e·mo·tion
e·mo·tion·al
em·per·or
em·pha·sis
em·pha·size
em·phat·ic
em·pire

em·ploy
em·ploy·ee
em·ploy·er
em·ploy·ment
em·pow·er
emp·ti·ness
emp·ty
e·mul·sion
en·a·ble
en·act
e·nam·el
en·am·ored
en·camp
en·case
en·chant
en·close
en·clo·sure
en·core
en·coun·ter
en·cour·age
en·cum·ber
en·cy·clo·pe·di·a
en·dan·ger
en·dear
en·deav·or
en·dem·ic
en·do·crine
en·dorse
en·dow·ment
en·dur·ance
en·dure
en·e·my
en·er·get·ic
en·er·gy
en·fold
en·force
en·gage
en·gine
en·gi·neer
Eng·lish
en·grave
en·grav·ing
en·gross
en·hance

e·nig·ma
en·joy
en·large
en·light·en
en·list
en·mi·ty
en·no·ble
e·nor·mous
e·nough
en·rage
en·rich
en·roll
en·sem·ble
en·sign
en·slave
en·snare
en·sue
en·tail
en·tan·gle
en·ter
en·ter·prise
en·ter·pris·ing
en·ter·tain
en·thu·si·asm
en·thu·si·ast
en·thu·si·as·tic
en·tice
en·tire
en·ti·tle
en·ti·ty
en·trails
en·trance
en·treat
en·trust
en·try
e·nu·mer·ate
en·vel·op
en·ve·lope
en·vi·a·ble
en·vi·ous
en·vi·ron·ment
en·vis·age
en·vy
en·zyme

ep·ic
ep·i·dem·ic
E·pis·co·pal
ep·i·sode
ep·i·taph
e·pit·o·me
ep·och
e·qual
e·qual·i·ty
e·qua·tion
e·qua·tor
e·qui·lib·ri·um
e·quip
e·quip·ment
eq·ui·ta·ble
eq·ui·ty
e·quiv·a·lent
e·quiv·o·cal
er·a
e·rad·i·cate
e·rase
e·rect
e·rec·tion
e·rode
e·ro·sion
err
er·rand
er·rat·ic
er·ro·ne·ous
er·ror
e·rup·tion
es·ca·late
es·ca·la·tor
es·cape
es·chew
es·cort
es·crow
es·pi·o·nage
es·say
es·sence
es·sen·tial
es·tab·lish
es·tate
es·teem

es·ti·mate
es·ti·ma·tion
e·ter·nal
e·ter·ni·ty
e·the·re·al
eth·i·cal
eth·ics
eth·nic
eu·tha·na·sia
e·vac·u·ate
e·vac·u·a·tion
e·vade
e·val·u·ate
e·val·u·a·tion
e·van·gel·i·cal
e·vap·o·rate
e·va·sion
e·ven
eve·ning
e·vent
e·ven·tu·al·i·ty
e·ven·tu·al·ly
ev·er
ev·er·green
eve·ry
eve·ry·bod·y
eve·ry·day
eve·ry·one
eve·ry·thing
eve·ry·where
e·vic·tion
ev·i·dence
ev·i·dent
e·vil
ev·o·lu·tion
ex·act
ex·ag·ger·ate
ex·alt
ex·am·i·na·tion
ex·am·ine
ex·am·ple
ex·as·per·ate
ex·ca·vate
ex·ceed

ex·cel
ex·cel·lence
ex·cel·lent
ex·cept
ex·cep·tion
ex·cerpt
ex·cess
ex·ces·sive
ex·change
ex·cise
ex·cite
ex·cit·ing
ex·claim
ex·cla·ma·tion
ex·clude
ex·clu·sive
ex·cre·tion
ex·cur·sion
ex·cuse
ex·e·cute
ex·e·cu·tion
ex·ec·u·tive
ex·ec·u·tor
ex·empt
ex·emp·tion
ex·er·cise
ex·ert
ex·er·tion
ex·hale
ex·haust
ex·haus·tion
ex·haus·tive
ex·hib·it
ex·hi·bi·tion
ex·hil·a·rate
ex·hort
ex·ile
ex·ist
ex·ist·ence
ex·it
ex·or·bi·tant
ex·ot·ic
ex·pand
ex·panse

ex·pan·sion
ex·pan·sive
ex·pect
ex·pect·ant
ex·pec·ta·tion
ex·pe·di·tion
ex·pel
ex·pend
ex·pend·i·ture
ex·pense
ex·pen·sive
ex·pe·ri·ence
ex·per·i·ment
ex·per·i·men·tal
ex·pert
ex·pi·ra·tion
ex·pire
ex·plain
ex·pla·na·tion
ex·ploit
ex·ploi·ta·tion
ex·plo·ra·tion
ex·plore
ex·plor·er
ex·plo·sion
ex·plo·sive
ex·po·nent
ex·port
ex·pose
ex·po·sure
ex·press
ex·pres·sion
ex·pres·sive
ex·pro·pri·ate
ex·pul·sion
ex·qui·site
ex·tend
ex·ten·sion
ex·ten·sive
ex·tent
ex·te·ri·or
ex·ter·mi·nate
ex·ter·nal
ex·tinct

ex·tinc·tion
ex·tin·guish
ex·tort
ex·tor·tion
ex·tra
ex·tract
ex·trac·tion
ex·tra·ne·ous
ex·traor·di·nar·y
ex·trav·a·gance
ex·trav·a·gant
ex·treme
ex·trem·i·ty
ex·tro·vert
eye
eye·ball
eye·brow
eye·glass·es
eye·lash
eye·lid
eye·sight
eye·wit·ness

F

fa·ble
fab·ric
fab·ri·cate
fab·u·lous
face
fa·cial
fac·ile
fa·cil·i·ty
fact
fac·tion
fac·tor
fac·to·ry
fac·tu·al
fac·ul·ty
fade
fail
fail·ure
faint
fair

fair·way
fair·y
faith
faith·ful
faith·less
fake
fal·con
fall
fal·la·cy
fall·en
fal·li·ble
fall·out
fal·low
false
false·hood
fal·si·fi·ca·tion
fal·si·fy
fal·ter
fame
fa·mil·iar
fa·mil·iar·i·ty
fa·mil·iar·ize
fam·i·ly
fam·ine
fam·ish
fa·mous
fa·nat·ic
fan·ci·ful
fan·cy
fan·fare
fan·tas·tic
fan·ta·sy
farce
fare
fare·well
farm
farm·er
farm·house
farm·yard
far-off
far-reach·ing
far-sight·ed
far·ther
far·thest

fas·ci·nate
fas·cism
fash·ion
fast
fas·ten
fas·tid·i·ous
fa·tal
fate
fa·ther
fa·tigue
fau·cet
fault
fault·y
fa·vor
fa·vor·a·ble
fa·vor·ite
fawn
fear
fear·ful
fea·si·ble
feast
feat
feath·er
fea·ture
fed·er·al
fed·e·ra·tion
fee·ble
feed
feed·back
feed·er
feel
feel·ing
feet
feign
feint
fe·lic·i·tate
fe·line
fell
fel·low
fel·low·ship
fel·on
fel·o·ny
felt
fe·male

fem·i·nine
fence
fend·er
fer·ment
fern
fe·ro·cious
fer·ry
fer·tile
fer·til·i·ty
fer·ti·lize
fer·ti·liz·er
fer·vent
fer·vid
fer·vor
fes·ter
fes·ti·val
fes·tive
fete
fe·tish
fet·ter
fe·tus
feud
fe·ver
few
fi·as·co
fi·ber
fic·tion
fic·ti·tious
fid·dle
fi·del·i·ty
fidg·et
field
field trip
fiend
fiend·ish
fierce
fie·ry
fi·es·ta
fif·teen
fifth
fif·ti·eth
fif·ty
fight
fight·er

fig·ment
fig·ur·a·tive
fig·ure
fig·ure·head
fil·a·ment
file
fi·let
fil·i·bus·ter
fill
fill·er
fil·let
film
film·strip
fil·ter
filth
filth·y
fil·tra·tion
fi·nal
fi·na·le
fi·nal·ly
fi·nance
fi·nan·cial
fin·an·cier
find
fine
fin·ger
fin·ger·print
fin·ish
fi·nite
fire
fire·arm
fire en·gine
fire es·cape
fire·fly
fire·house
fire·man
fire·place
fire·proof
fire·side
fire·trap
fire·wood
fire·works
firm
fir·ma·ment

first
first aid
first-born
first class
first la·dy
fis·cal
fish
fish·er·man
fish·er·y
fish·hook
fis·sion
fis·sure
fist
five
fix·ture
fiz·zle
flag
flag·pole
fla·grant
flair
flake
flam·boy·ant
flame
flam·ma·ble
flank
flan·nel
flap
flare
flash
flash·back
flash·bulb
flash·light
flask
flat
flat·ten
flat·ter
flat·ter·y
flaunt
fla·vor
flaw
flax
flea
flee
fleece

fleet
flesh
flesh·y
flew
flex·i·ble
flick·er
fli·er
flight
flim·sy
fling
flint
flint·y
flip
flip·pant
flirt
float
flock
flood
flood·light
flood·wa·ter
floor
floor·ing
flop
flo·ral
flor·id
flo·rist
flounce
floun·der
flour
flour·ish
flout
flow
flow·er
flow·er·y
flown
flu
fluc·tu·ate
flu·ent
flu·id
flung
flu·o·res·cent
fluor·i·date
flu·o·ride
flur·ry

flush
flute
flut·ter
fly
foam
foam rub·ber
fo·cus
fod·der
fog·gy
foil
fold
fold·er
fo·li·age
folk
folk·lore
folk song
fol·low
fol·low·er
fol·ly
fond
food
fool
fool·ish
fool·proof
foot
foot·ball
foot·hill
foot·lights
foot·print
foot·step
foot·stool
for
for·age
for·bade
for·bear
for·bear·ance
for·bid
for·bid·den
force
for·ci·ble
ford
fore·arm
fore·cast
fore·clo·sure

fore·fa·ther
fore·front
fore·gone
fore·hand
fore·head
for·eign
for·eign·er
fore·man
fore·most
fore·run·ner
fore·see
fore·shad·ow
fore·sight
for·est
for·est·ry
fore·tell
fore·thought
for·ev·er
fore·warn
fore·word
for·feit
for·ger·y
for·get
for·give
for·go
for·gone
fork
for·lorn
form
for·mal
for·ma·tion
for·mer
for·mi·da·ble
for·mu·la
for·sake
fort
forth
forth·com·ing
forth·right
for·ti·eth
for·ti·fi·ca·tion
for·ti·fy
fort·night
for·tress

for·tu·nate
for·tune
for·ty
fo·rum
for·ward
fos·sil
fos·ter
fought
foul
found
foun·da·tion
foun·der
found·ry
foun·tain
four
four·teen
fourth
fowl
foy·er
frac·tion
frac·ture
frag·ment
fra·grance
fra·grant
frail
frame
frame-up
frame·work
fran·chise
frank
frank·furt·er
fran·tic
fra·ter·nal
fra·ter·ni·ty
fraud
fraud·u·lent
fraught
fray
freak
freck·le
free
free·dom
freeze
freez·er

freight
fren·zy
fre·quen·cy
fre·quent
fresh
fresh·man
fresh·wa·ter
fret
fri·ar
fric·tion
fried
friend
friend·ship
fright
fright·en
fright·ful
frig·id
frisk·y
friv·o·lous
frock
frog
frog·man
frol·ic
front
fron·tier
frost
froth
frown
froze
fro·zen
fru·gal
fruit
fruit·ful
fru·i·tion
frus·trate
fry
fudge
fu·el
fu·gi·tive
ful·fill
full·back
ful·ly
fum·ble
fume

func·tion
fund
fun·da·men·tal
fu·ner·al
fun·gus
fun·nel
fun·ny
fur
fu·ri·ous
fur·nace
fur·nish
fur·ni·ture
fur·or
fur·ry
fur·ther
fur·ther·more
fu·ry
fuse
fu·sion
fuss
fu·tile
fu·til·i·ty
fu·ture

G

gadg·et
gage
gai·e·ty
gai·ly
gain
gal·ax·y
gale
gall
gal·lant
gal·lant·ry
gal·ler·y
gal·ley
gal·lon
gal·lop
gal·lows
gal·va·nize
gam·ble
game

gam·ma glob·u·lin
gam·ut
gang
gang·plank
gan·grene
gang·ster
gang·way
ga·rage
garb
gar·bage
gar·den
gar·gle
gar·land
gar·lic
gar·ment
gar·ner
gar·nish
gar·nish·ee
gar·ret
gar·ri·son
gar·ter
gas·e·ous
gash
gas·ket
gas·o·line
gasp
gas·tric
gate
gate·way
gath·er
gaud·y
gauge
gaunt
gaunt·let
gauze
gave
gav·el
gay
gaze
gear
gear·shift
geese
gel·a·tin
gen·der

gene
ge·ne·al·o·gy
gen·er·al
gen·er·al·i·za·tion
gen·er·al·ize
gen·er·ate
gen·er·a·tion
gen·e·ra·tor
gen·er·os·i·ty
gen·er·ous
ge·net·ic
gen·ial
gen·ius
gen·tle
gen·tle·man
gen·tle·wom·an
gen·tly
gen·u·ine
ge·o·graph·i·cal
ge·og·ra·phy
ge·o·log·i·cal
ge·ol·o·gy
ge·o·met·ric
ge·om·e·try
ge·o·phys·i·cal
ge·o·phys·ics
ger·i·at·rics
germ
ger·mane
ger·mi·nate
ger·mi·na·tion
ges·ta·tion
ges·tic·u·late
ges·ture
get-to·geth·er
gey·ser
ghast·ly
ghet·to
ghost
gi·ant
gib·ber·ish
gid·dy
gift
gi·gan·tic

gig·gle
gill
gim·mick
gin·ger
gin·ger·bread
ging·ham
gi·raffe
gird
gir·dle
girl
giv·en
giv·er
gla·cial
gla·cier
glad·den
glade
glam·or·ous
glam·our
glance
gland
glan·du·lar
glare
glar·ing
glass
glass·y
glau·co·ma
glaze
gleam
glean
glee
glide
glid·er
glim·mer
glimpse
glis·ten
glit·ter
glob·al
globe
glob·ule
gloom
glo·ri·fy
glo·ri·ous
glo·ry
gloss

glove
glow
glu·cose
glue
glut·ton
glyc·er·in
gnash
gnat
gnaw
goad
goal
goal·keep·er
goat
gob·ble
go-be·tween
gob·let
gob·lin
god·dess
god·fa·ther
god·like
god·ly
god·moth·er
god·par·ent
god·send
goes
go·ing
goi·ter
gold·en
gold·en·rod
gold-filled
gold·fish
golf
gone
gong
good-by
good·li·ness
good-look·ing
good-na·tured
good-sized
good will
goose
gore
gorge
gor·geous

go·ril·la
gor·y
gos·pel
gos·sip
got·ten
gouge
gourd
gour·met
gov·ern
gov·ern·ment
gov·er·nor
gown
grab
grace
grace·ful
gra·cious
grade
gra·di·ent
grad·u·al
grad·u·ate
grad·u·a·tion
graft
grain
gram
gram·mar
gram·mat·i·cal
gran·ar·y
grand
grand·child
grand·daugh·ter
gran·deur
grand·fa·ther
gran·di·ose
grand·moth·er
grand·par·ent
grand·son
grand·stand
gran·ite
grant
gran·u·lar
gran·u·late
grape
grape·fruit
grape·vine

graph
graph·ic
graph·ite
grap·ple
grasp
grass
grass·hop·per
grass roots
grate
grate·ful
grat·i·fi·ca·tion
grat·i·fy
grat·i·tude
grave
grav·el
grav·i·tate
grav·i·ta·tion
grav·i·ty
gra·vy
gray
graze
grease
great
greed
greed·i·ness
greed·y
green
green·house
green·ness
greet
gre·gar·i·ous
gre·nade
grew
grey
grey·hound
grid
grid·dle
grief
griev·ance
grieve
griev·ous
grill
grille
grim

grime
grim·y
grin
grind
grind·stone
grip
gripe
grit
groan
gro·cer
gro·cer·y
grog·gy
groin
groom
groove
grope
gross
gro·tesque
grouch
ground
ground·work
group
grove
grow
growl
grown
growth
grub
grudge
gru·el
gru·el·ing
grue·some
grum·ble
grunt
guar·an·tee
guar·an·tor
guar·an·ty
guard
guard·i·an
guer·ril·la
guess
guess·work
guest
guest·house

guid·ance
guide
guide·book
guide·post
guild
guile
guilt
guilt·y
guin·ea
gui·tar
gulf
gull
gul·ly
gulp
gum·drop
gun·fire
gun·pow·der
gun·shot
gun·smith
gur·gle
gush
gust
gut·ter
gym
gym·nas·tics
gyp·sy

H

hab·it
hab·it·a·ble
hab·i·ta·tion
ha·bit·u·al
hack
had·dock
hag·gard
hag·gle
hail
hail·stone
hair
hair·cut
hair·dress·er
hair·pin
hair's-breadth

hair·split·ting
hair·y
hale
half
half·back
half·way
hal·i·but
hall
hall·mark
Hal·low·een
hal·lu·ci·na·tion
hall·way
halt
hal·ter
halve
ham·burg·er
ham·let
ham·mer
ham·mock
ham·per
hand·bag
hand·ball
hand·book
hand·cuff
hand·ful
hand·i·cap
hand·i·work
hand·ker·chief
han·dle
hand·made
hand·out
hand·rail
hand·shake
hand·some
hand·writ·ing
hand·y
hand·y·man
hang
hang·ar
hang·er
hang·nail
hang·out
hang·o·ver
hap·haz·ard

hap·less
hap·pen
hap·pi·ly
hap·pi·ness
hap·py
ha·rangue
har·ass
har·bor
hard
hard·en
hard-head·ed
hard-heart·ed
hard·ly
hard·ship
hard·top
hard·ware
hard·wood
har·dy
hare
harm
harm·ful
harm·less
har·mo·ni·ous
har·mo·nize
har·mo·ny
har·ness
harp
har·poon
har·row
har·ry
harsh
har·vest
hash·ish
haste
has·ten
hast·i·ly
hast·y
hatch
hatch·et
hate
hate·ful
ha·tred
haugh·ty
haul

haunch
haunt
haunt·ed
have
ha·ven
hav·oc
hawk
haw·thorn
hay
hay fe·ver
hay·stack
hay·wire
haz·ard
haz·ard·ous
haze
ha·zel
ha·zy
head
head·ache
head·first
head·light
head·line
head·long
head-on
head·phone
head·quar·ters
head·stone
head·strong
head·wait·er
head·way
heal
health
health·ful
health·y
heap
hear
heard
hear·ing aid
hear·say
hearse
heart
heart·beat
heart·bro·ken
heart·felt

hearth
heart·i·ly
heart·y
heat
heat·er
heath
hea·then
heath·er
heave
heav·en
heav·en·ly
heav·i·ly
heav·i·ness
heav·y·weight
hec·tare
hec·tic
hedge
hedge·hog
heed
heed·less
heel
height
hei·nous
heir
heir·loom
held
hel·i·cop·ter
hel·i·port
he·li·um
hell·ish
hel·lo
helm
hel·met
helms·man
help
help·er
help·ful
help·less
hem·i·sphere
hem·lock
he·mo·glo·bin
hem·or·rhage
hemp
hence

hence·forth
her·ald
herb
herd
herds·man
here
here·af·ter
here·by
he·red·i·tar·y
he·red·i·ty
here·in
her·e·sy
her·e·tic
here·to·fore
here·with
her·it·age
her·met·i·cal·ly
her·mit
her·ni·a
he·ro
he·ro·ic
her·o·in
her·o·ine
her·o·ism
her·ring
hes·i·tate
hes·i·ta·tion
het·er·o·ge·ne·ous
hew
hi·ber·nate
hic·cup
hick·o·ry
hid·den
hide
hid·e·ous
hide·out
hi·er·ar·chy
hi·er·o·glyph·ics
high
high fi·del·i·ty
high·lands
high·light
high-mind·ed
high-pitched

high-pow·ered
high-pres·sure
high school
high·way
hi·jack
hike
hi·lar·i·ous
hill·bil·ly
hill·side
hill·top
hill·y
hilt
hind
hin·der
hin·drance
hinge
hint
hire
hiss
his·to·ri·an
his·tor·ic
his·tor·i·cal
his·tor·y
hit-and-run
hitch
hitch·hike
hith·er
hith·er·to
hive
hoard
hoarse
hoar·y
hoax
hob·ble
hob·by
hock·ey
hoe
hoist
hold
hold·er
hole
hol·i·day
ho·li·ness
hol·low

hol·ly
hol·o·caust
ho·ly
hom·age
home
home·less
home·ly
home·made
home run
home·sick
home·ward
home·work
hom·i·cide
ho·mo·ge·ne·ous
ho·mog·e·nize
hon·est
hon·es·ty
hon·ey
hon·ey·comb
hon·ey·moon
hon·or
hon·or·a·ble
hon·or·ar·y
hood
hood·lum
hoof
hook
hook·up
hoop
hoot
hope
hope·ful
hope·less
hop·per
horde
ho·ri·zon
ho·ri·zon·tal
hor·mone
horn
hor·net
ho·ro·scope
hor·ri·ble
hor·rid
hor·ri·fy

hor·ror
horse
horse·back
horse·hair
horse·man
horse·play
horse·pow·er
horse·shoe
hor·ti·cul·ture
hose
ho·sier·y
hos·pi·ta·ble
hos·pi·tal
hos·pi·tal·i·ty
hos·pi·tal·ize
host
hos·tage
hos·tel
host·ess
hos·tile
hos·til·i·ty
ho·tel
hot-head·ed
hot·house
hound
hour
hour·ly
house
house·boat
house·break·ing
house·bro·ken
house·fly
house·hold
house·keep·er
house·maid
house·top
house·wife
house·work
hov·el
hov·er
how·ev·er
howl
hub·cap
hud·dle

hue
huff
huge
hulk
hull
hu·man
hu·mane
hu·man·i·tar·i·an
hu·man·i·ty
hum·ble
hum·bug
hu·mid
hu·mid·i·ty
hu·mil·i·ate
hu·mil·i·a·tion
hu·mil·i·ty
hu·mor
hu·mor·ous
hunch
hun·dred
hun·dredth
hung
hun·ger
hun·gry
hunt
hunt·er
hur·dle
hurl
hur·ri·cane
hur·ried
hur·ry
hurt
hurt·ful
hus·band
hush
husk·y
hus·tle
hy·brid
hy·drant
hy·drau·lic
hy·dro·car·bon
hy·dro·e·lec·tric
hy·dro·foil
hy·dro·gen

hy·dro·pho·bi·a
hy·e·na
hy·gi·en·ic
hy·gien·ist
hymn
hy·per·bo·le
hy·per·sen·si·tive
hy·per·ten·sion
hy·phen
hy·phen·a·tion
hyp·no·sis
hyp·not·ic
hyp·no·tize
hy·po·chon·dri·ac
hy·poc·ri·sy
hyp·o·crite
hy·po·der·mic
hy·poth·e·sis
hy·po·thet·i·cal
hys·te·ri·a
hys·ter·i·cal

I

ice
ice·berg
ice·break·er
ice cream
ice skate
i·ci·cle
i·cy
i·de·a
i·de·al
i·den·ti·cal
i·den·ti·fi·ca·tion
i·den·ti·fy
i·de·o·log·i·cal
i·de·ol·o·gy
id·i·o·cy
id·i·om
id·i·ot
i·dle
i·dol
i·dol·a·try

i·dol·ize
ig·nite
ig·ni·tion
ig·no·min·i·ous
ig·no·rance
ig·no·rant
ig·nore
il·le·gal
il·le·git·i·mate
ill-fat·ed
il·lic·it
il·lit·er·a·cy
il·lit·er·ate
ill·ness
il·lu·mi·nate
il·lu·sion
il·lus·trate
il·lus·tra·tion
im·age
i·mag·i·na·ble
i·mag·i·na·tion
i·mag·i·na·tive
i·mag·ine
im·be·cile
im·i·tate
im·i·ta·tion
im·ma·te·ri·al
im·ma·ture
im·ma·tu·ri·ty
im·meas·ur·a·ble
im·me·di·ate
im·mense
im·merse
im·mi·grant
im·mi·grate
im·mi·gra·tion
im·mi·nent
im·mo·bi·lize
im·mo·ral
im·mor·tal
im·mov·a·ble
im·mune
im·mu·ni·ty
im·mu·ni·za·tion

im·mu·ta·ble
im·pair
im·pan·el
im·part
im·par·tial
im·pass·a·ble
im·pa·tience
im·pa·tient
im·peach
im·pede
im·pel
im·pend·ing
im·pen·e·tra·ble
im·per·a·tive
im·per·cep·ti·ble
im·per·fect
im·per·fec·tion
im·pe·ri·al
im·per·il
im·pe·ri·ous
im·per·me·a·ble
im·per·son·al
im·per·son·ate
im·per·ti·nence
im·per·ti·nent
im·pet·u·ous
im·pe·tus
im·pla·ca·ble
im·plant
im·ple·ment
im·pli·cate
im·pli·ca·tion
im·plic·it
im·plore
im·ply
im·po·lite
im·port
im·por·tance
im·por·tant
im·por·ta·tion
im·port·er
im·pose
im·po·si·tion
im·pos·si·ble

im·pos·tor
im·po·tent
im·pound
im·pov·er·ish
im·prac·ti·cal
im·preg·na·ble
im·press
im·pres·sion
im·pres·sive
im·print
im·pris·on
im·prob·a·ble
im·prop·er
im·prove
im·pro·vise
im·pru·dent
im·pu·dent
im·pugn
im·pulse
im·pul·sive
im·pu·ni·ty
im·pure
in·a·bil·i·ty
in·ac·ces·si·ble
in·ac·cur·ate
in·ac·tive
in·ad·e·quate
in·ad·mis·si·ble
in·ad·vert·ent
in·al·ien·a·ble
in·ap·pli·ca·ble
in·ap·pro·pri·ate
in·ar·tic·u·late
in·as·much
in·at·ten·tion
in·au·di·ble
in·au·gur·al
in·au·gu·rate
in·bred
in·cal·cu·la·ble
in·ca·pa·ble
in·ca·pac·i·tate
in·cen·di·ar·y
in·cense

in·ces·sant
in·ci·dence
in·ci·dent
in·ci·den·tal·ly
in·cin·er·a·tor
in·ci·sion
in·cite
in·cli·na·tion
in·cline
in·clude
in·clu·sion
in·clu·sive
in·co·her·ent
in·come
in·com·par·a·ble
in·com·pat·i·ble
in·com·pe·tent
in·com·plete
in·com·pre·hen·si·ble
in·con·ceiv·a·ble
in·con·clu·sive
in·con·gru·ous
in·con·se·quen·tial
in·con·sid·er·ate
in·con·sist·ent
in·con·spic·u·ous
in·con·ven·ience
in·con·ven·ient
in·cor·po·rate
in·cor·rect
in·cor·ri·gi·ble
in·cor·rupt·i·ble
in·crease
in·cred·i·ble
in·cred·u·lous
in·cre·ment
in·cu·ba·tor
in·cum·bent
in·cur
in·cur·a·ble
in·de·cent
in·de·ci·sive
in·deed
in·def·i·nite

in·del·i·ble
in·dem·ni·fy
in·dem·ni·ty
in·dent
in·de·pend·ence
in·de·pend·ent
in·de·struct·i·ble
in·dex
in·di·cate
in·di·ca·tion
in·dic·a·tive
in·di·ca·tor
in·dict·ment
in·dif·fer·ence
in·dif·fer·ent
in·dig·e·nous
in·di·ges·tion
in·dig·nant
in·dig·ni·ty
in·di·rect
in·dis·cre·tion
in·dis·crim·i·nate
in·dis·pen·sa·ble
in·dis·put·a·ble
in·dis·tinct
in·di·vid·u·al
in·di·vis·i·ble
in·do·lence
in·do·lent
in·doors
in·duce
in·duce·ment
in·duct
in·duc·tive
in·dulge
in·dul·gence
in·dus·tri·al
in·dus·tri·al·ize
in·dus·tri·ous
in·dus·try
in·ef·fec·tive
in·ef·fi·cient
in·el·i·gi·ble
in·e·qual·i·ty

in·eq·ui·ta·ble
in·er·tia
in·es·cap·a·ble
in·es·ti·ma·ble
in·ev·i·ta·ble
in·ex·haust·i·ble
in·ex·o·ra·ble
in·ex·pen·sive
in·ex·pe·ri·enced
in·ex·pli·ca·ble
in·fal·li·ble
in·fa·mous
in·fa·my
in·fan·cy
in·fant
in·fan·try
in·fect
in·fec·tion
in·fec·tious
in·fer
in·fe·ri·or
in·fer·nal
in·fest
in·fi·del·i·ty
in·fil·trate
in·fi·nite
in·fin·i·ty
in·firm
in·fir·ma·ry
in·flame
in·flam·ma·ble
in·flam·ma·tion
in·flate
in·fla·tion
in·flex·i·ble
in·flict
in·flu·ence
in·flu·en·tial
in·form
in·for·mal
in·for·ma·tion
in·fringe
in·fur·i·ate
in·fu·sion

in·gen·ious
in·ge·nu·i·ty
in·grained
in·grat·i·tude
in·gre·di·ent
in·hab·it
in·hab·it·ant
in·hale
in·her·ent
in·her·it
in·her·it·ance
in·hi·bi·tion
in·hos·pi·ta·ble
in·hu·man
in·im·i·cal
in·iq·ui·ty
i·ni·tial
i·ni·ti·ate
i·ni·ti·a·tive
in·jec·tion
in·junc·tion
in·jure
in·ju·ri·ous
in·jur·y
in·jus·tice
ink
in·laid
in·land
in·lay
in·let
in·mate
inn
in·ner
in·ning
in·no·cence
in·no·cent
in·noc·u·ous
in·no·va·tion
in·nu·en·do
in·nu·mer·a·ble
in·oc·u·la·tion
in·of·fen·sive
in·or·gan·ic
in·quest

in·quire
in·quir·y
in·quis·i·tive
in·sane
in·san·i·ty
in·sa·tia·ble
in·scribe
in·scrip·tion
in·sect
in·se·cure
in·sen·si·ble
in·sen·si·tive
in·sep·a·ra·ble
in·sert
in·ser·tion
in·side
in·sight
in·sig·ni·a
in·sig·nif·i·cant
in·sin·u·ate
in·sist
in·sist·ent
in·sole
in·so·lence
in·so·lent
in·sol·u·ble
in·som·ni·a
in·spec·tion
in·spec·tor
in·spi·ra·tion
in·spire
in·stall
in·stal·la·tion
in·stall·ment
in·stance
in·stant
in·stan·ta·ne·ous
in·stead
in·sti·gate
in·still
in·stinct
in·sti·tute
in·sti·tu·tion
in·struct

in·struc·tion
in·struc·tor
in·stru·ment
in·suf·fer·a·ble
in·suf·fi·cient
in·su·late
in·su·la·tion
in·su·lin
in·sult
in·sur·ance
in·sure
in·sur·gent
in·sur·mount·a·ble
in·sur·rec·tion
in·tan·gi·ble
in·te·gral
in·te·grate
in·te·gra·tion
in·teg·ri·ty
in·tel·lect
in·tel·lec·tu·al
in·tel·li·gence
in·tel·li·gent
in·tend
in·tense
in·ten·si·fy
in·ten·si·ty
in·tent
in·ten·tion
in·ter
in·ter·cede
in·ter·cept
in·ter·change
in·ter·com
in·ter·course
in·ter·est
in·ter·fere
in·ter·fer·ence
in·ter·im
in·te·ri·or
in·ter·ject
in·ter·lock
in·ter·lude
in·ter·me·di·ate

in·ter·mis·sion
in·ter·mit·tent
in·ter·nal
in·ter·na·tion·al
in·ter·pret
in·ter·pre·ta·tion
in·ter·pret·er
in·ter·ro·gate
in·ter·rupt
in·ter·rup·tion
in·ter·sec·tion
in·ter·state
in·ter·val
in·ter·vene
in·ter·view
in·tes·ti·nal
in·tes·tine
in·ti·mate
in·tim·i·date
in·tol·er·a·ble
in·tol·er·ance
in·to·na·tion
in·tox·i·cate
in·tra·ve·nous
in·tri·cate
in·trigue
in·trin·sic
in·tro·duce
in·tro·duc·tion
in·trude
in·tru·sion
in·tu·i·tion
in·un·date
in·vade
in·va·lid
in·val·u·a·ble
in·var·i·a·ble
in·va·sion
in·vent
in·ven·tion
in·ven·tor
in·ven·to·ry
in·vert
in·vest

in·ves·ti·gate
in·ves·ti·ga·tion
in·vest·ment
in·vet·er·ate
in·vig·or·ate
in·vin·ci·ble
in·vis·i·ble
in·vi·ta·tion
in·vite
in·voice
in·vol·un·tar·y
in·volve
in·ward
i·on
ire
i·ris
irk·some
i·ron
i·ron·ic
i·ro·ny
ir·ra·tion·al
ir·ref·u·ta·ble
ir·reg·u·lar
ir·rel·e·vant
ir·rep·a·ra·ble
ir·re·place·a·ble
ir·re·proach·a·ble
ir·re·sist·i·ble
ir·re·spon·si·ble
ir·re·vers·i·ble
ir·rev·o·ca·ble
ir·ri·gate
ir·ri·ga·tion
ir·ri·ta·ble
ir·ri·tate
is·land
isle
i·so·late
i·so·la·tion
is·sue
i·tal·ic
itch
i·tem
i·tem·ize

i·tin·er·ar·y
it·self
i·vor·y
i·vy

J

jack
jack·al
jack·et
jack·knife
jack·pot
jade
jail
jail·er
jam
jan·i·tor
jar·gon
jaun·dice
jaun·ty
jay·walk
jazz
jeal·ous
jeal·ous·y
jeep
jeer
jel·ly
jeop·ard·y
jerk
jer·sey
jest
jew·el
jew·el·er
jew·el·ry
jig·saw
jin·gle
jinx
jock·ey
joc·u·lar
jog·ger
join
join·er
joint
joke

jol·ly
jolt
jos·tle
jour·nal
jour·nal·ist
jour·ney
jo·vi·al
joy·ful
joy·ous
ju·bi·lant
ju·bi·lee
judge
judg·ment
ju·di·cial
ju·di·ci·ar·y
ju·di·cious
jug·gle
juice
juic·y
jum·ble
jump
junc·tion
jun·gle
jun·ior
ju·ni·per
ju·ris·dic·tion
ju·ror
ju·ry
just
jus·tice
jus·ti·fi·a·ble
jus·ti·fi·ca·tion
jus·ti·fy
ju·ve·nile
jux·ta·po·si·tion

K

ka·lei·do·scope
kan·ga·roo
ka·pok
kar·at
ka·ra·te

kay·ak
keel
keen
keep
keep·er
ken·nel
kept
ker·nel
ker·o·sene
ketch·up
ket·tle
key·board
key·hole
key·note
kick
kick·back
kick·off
kid·nap
kid·ney
ki·lo
kil·o·gram
kil·o·li·ter
kil·o·me·ter
kil·o·ton
kil·o·watt
ki·mo·no
kind
kin·der·gar·ten
kin·dle
kind·ly
kind·ness
kin·dred
king
king·dom
kins·man
ki·osk
kiss
kitch·en
kite
kit·ten
knack
knave
knead
knee

kneel
knell
knelt
knew
knife
knight
knit
knives
knob
knock
knock·out
knoll
knot
know
knowl·edge
knowl·edge·a·ble
known
knuck·le
ko·sher

L

la·bel
la·bor
lab·o·ra·to·ry
la·bor·er
la·bo·ri·ous
lace
lac·er·a·tion
lack
lac·quer
lad·der
lad·en
la·dle
la·dy
laid
lain
lake
lamb
lame
la·ment
lamp
lance
land

land·lord
land·mark
land·scape
lane
lan·guage
lan·o·lin
lan·tern
lapse
lar·ce·ny
lard
large
large-scale
lark
lar·va
las·civ·i·ous
la·ser
lash
last
latch
late
la·tent
lathe
lath·er
lat·i·tude
lat·ter
laugh
laugh·ter
launch
laun·der
laun·dry
lau·rel
la·va
lav·a·to·ry
lav·ish
law
law-a·bid·ing
law·ful
lawn
lawn mow·er
law·suit
law·yer
lax·a·tive
lay
lay·er

lay·man
lay·off
lay·out
la·zy
lead
lead·er·ship
leaf
leaf·let
leaf·y
league
leak
lean
leap
learn
lease
least
leath·er
leave
leaves
lec·ture
lec·tur·er
led
ledge
ledg·er
leek
leer
lee·way
left
left-hand·ed
left·o·ver
leg·a·cy
le·gal
le·gal·ize
leg·end
leg·end·ar·y
leg·i·ble
le·gion
leg·is·late
leg·is·la·tion
leg·is·la·tive
leg·is·la·tor
leg·is·la·ture
le·git·i·mate
lei·sure

lem·on
lem·on·ade
lend
length
length·en
len·ient
lens
lent
leop·ard
less
less·en
less·er
les·son
lest
le·thal
let·ter
let·tuce
leu·ke·mi·a
lev·el
lev·er
lev·er·age
lev·y
lewd
li·a·bil·i·ty
li·a·ble
li·ar
li·bel
lib·er·al
lib·er·ate
lib·er·ty
li·brar·i·an
li·brar·y
li·cense
lick
lie
lieu·ten·ant
life
life·guard
life·like
life·long
life-size
life·time
lift
lig·a·ment

light
light·en
light-head·ed
light·house
light·ning
light·weight
like
like·ly
lik·en
like·ness
like·wise
li·lac
lil·y
limb
lim·bo
lime
lim·it
lim·i·ta·tion
lim·ou·sine
limp
line
lin·e·ar
line·man
lin·en
line-up
lin·ger
lin·guis·tics
lin·i·ment
lin·ing
link
li·no·le·um
lin·seed
lint
li·on
li·on·ess
lip·stick
liq·ue·fy
liq·uid
liq·ui·date
liq·uor
lisp
list
lis·ten
lis·ten·er

list·less
li·ter
lit·er·a·cy
lit·er·al
lit·er·ar·y
lit·er·ate
lit·er·a·ture
lit·i·ga·tion
lit·ter
lit·tle
lit·ur·gy
live
live·li·hood
live·ly
liv·er
live·stock
liv·id
liv·ing
liz·ard
lla·ma
load
loaf
loan
loaves
lob·by
lob·by·ist
lob·ster
lo·cal
lo·cal·i·ty
lo·cal·ly
lo·cate
lo·ca·tion
lock
lock·er
lo·cust
lodge
lodg·ing
loft
loft·y
log·a·rithm
log·ic
log·i·cal
loin
loi·ter

lone
lone·li·ness
lone·ly
lone·some
lon·gi·tude
long-range
long·shore·man
look·out
loom
loop
loose
loos·en
lord
lore
lose
los·er
loss
lost
lo·tion
lot·ter·y
loud
lounge
louse
lov·a·ble
love
love·li·ness
love·ly
lov·er
low·er
low·li·ness
low·ly
loy·al
loy·al·ty
lu·bri·cant
lu·bri·cate
lu·bri·ca·tor
lu·cid
luck
luck·y
lu·cra·tive
lu·di·crous
luke·warm
lull
lum·ber

lu·mi·nous
lump
lu·nar
lu·na·tic
lunch
lunch·eon
lung
lunge
lure
lurk
lust
lus·ter
lust·y
lux·u·ri·ous
lux·ur·y
ly·ing
lymph
lym·phat·ic
lynx
lyr·ic

M

ma·chine
ma·chin·er·y
ma·chin·ist
mad·den
made
made-up
mad·man
mad·ness
mad·ras
mag·a·zine
mag·ic
mag·i·cal
ma·gi·cian
mag·is·trate
mag·net
mag·net·ic
mag·net·ize
mag·nif·i·cence
mag·nif·i·cent
mag·ni·fy
mag·ni·tude

ma·hog·a·ny
maid
maid·en
mail
mail·box
mail or·der
maim
main
main·land
main·stay
main·stream
main·tain
main·te·nance
ma·jes·tic
maj·es·ty
ma·jor
ma·jor·i·ty
make-be·lieve
mak·er
make·shift
make·up
mal·ad·just·ed
mal·a·dy
male
mal·func·tion
mal·ice
ma·li·cious
ma·lig·nant
mal·le·a·ble
mal·let
mal·nu·tri·tion
mal·prac·tice
malt
mam·mal
mam·moth
man·age
man·age·ment
man·ag·er
man·a·ge·ri·al
man·date
man·da·to·ry
mane
ma·neu·ver
man·ger

man·gle
man·hole
ma·ni·a
man·i·cure
man·i·fest
man·i·fes·ta·tion
man·i·fold
ma·nip·u·late
man·kind
man·ner
man·or
man·pow·er
man·sion
man·u·al
man·u·fac·ture
man·u·fac·tur·er
ma·nure
man·u·script
ma·ple
mar
mar·ble
march
mare
mar·gin
mar·gin·al
mar·i·jua·na
ma·rine
mar·i·ner
mar·i·tal
mar·i·time
mark
mar·ket
mar·ket·a·ble
mark·up
mar·ma·lade
ma·roon
mar·riage
mar·ried
mar·row
mar·ry
marsh
mar·shal
marsh·mal·low
mart

mar·tial
mar·tyr
mar·vel
mar·vel·ous
mas·cu·line
mash
mask
ma·son
ma·son·ry
mas·quer·ade
mass
mas·sa·cre
mas·sage
mas·sive
mast
mas·ter
mas·ter·piece
mas·ter·y
match
match·book
mate
ma·te·ri·al
ma·te·ri·al·ize
ma·ter·nal
ma·ter·ni·ty
math·e·mat·i·cal
math·e·mat·ics
mat·ri·mo·ny
ma·trix
ma·tron
mat·ter
mat·tress
mat·u·ra·tion
ma·ture
ma·tu·ri·ty
maul
max·i·mum
may·be
may·on·naise
may·or
maze
mead·ow
mea·ger
meal

meal·y
mean
me·an·der
meant
mean·time
mean·while
mea·sles
meas·ur·a·ble
meas·ure
meas·ure·ment
meat
me·chan·ic
me·chan·i·cal
mech·a·nism
mech·a·nize
med·al
med·dle
me·di·a
me·di·an
me·di·ate
me·di·a·tor
med·ic
med·i·cal
Med·i·care
med·i·cate
me·dic·i·nal
med·i·cine
me·di·e·val
me·di·o·cre
med·i·tate
med·i·ta·tion
me·di·um
med·ley
meek
meet
mel·an·chol·y
mel·low
me·lo·di·ous
mel·o·dra·ma
mel·o·dy
mel·on
melt
mem·ber
mem·ber·ship

mem·brane
mem·oir
mem·o·ra·ble
mem·o·ran·dum
me·mo·ri·al
mem·o·rize
mem·or·y
men·ace
me·nag·er·ie
mend
me·ni·al
men·tal
men·tal·i·ty
men·tion
men·u
mer·chan·dise
mer·chant
mer·ci·ful
mer·ci·less
mer·cu·ry
mer·cy
mere
merge
merg·er
me·ringue
mer·it
mer·i·to·ri·ous
mer·ri·ment
mer·ry
mesh
mess
mes·sage
mes·sen·ger
me·tab·o·lism
met·al
me·tal·lic
met·al·lur·gy
met·a·mor·pho·sis
met·a·phys·ics
me·te·or
me·te·or·o·log·i·cal
me·te·or·ol·o·gy
me·ter
meth·od

me·thod·i·cal
me·tic·u·lous
met·ric -
me·trop·o·lis
met·ro·pol·i·tan
mice
mi·cro·bi·ol·o·gy
mi·cro·film
mi·crom·e·ter
mi·cro·or·gan·ism
mi·cro·scope
mi·cro·wave
mid·day
mid·dle
mid·dle-class
mid·dle·man
midg·et
mid·land
mid·night
mid·way
mid·wife
mid·win·ter
mid·year
might
might·y
mi·grant
mi·grate
mi·gra·tion
mild
mil·dew
mile
mile·age
mil·i·tant
mil·i·ta·rist
mil·i·tar·y
mil·li·tia
milk
milk·man
milk shake
milk·y
mill
mil·len·ni·um
mill·er
mil·li·gram

mil·li·li·ter
mil·li·ner·y
mil·lion
mil·lion·aire
mime
mim·ic
mince
mind
mind·less
mine
min·er
min·er·al
min·er·a·log·i·cal
min·er·al·o·gy
min·gle
min·i·a·ture
min·i·mal
min·i·mum
min·is·ter
min·is·try
min·now
mi·nor
mi·nor·i·ty
min·strel
mint
mi·nus
min·ute
mir·a·cle
mi·rac·u·lous
mi·rage
mir·ror
mis·ap·pre·hen·sion
mis·ap·pro·pri·a·tion
mis·be·have
mis·cal·cu·late
mis·car·riage
mis·cel·la·ne·ous
mis·chance
mis·chief
mis·chie·vou
mis·con·cep·tion
mis·de·mean·or
mi·ser
mis·er·a·ble

mis·er·y
mis·fire
mis·fit
mis·for·tune
mis·giv·ing
mis·guid·ed
mis·hap
mis·in·ter·pret
mis·lead
mis·led
mis·place
mis·pro·nounce
miss
mis·sile
mis·sion
mis·sion·ar·y
mis·spell
mist
mis·take
mis·tak·en
mis·tress
mis·tri·al
mis·trust
mist·y
mis·un·der·stand
mis·un·der·stood
mis·use
mit·i·gate
mitt
mit·ten
mix
mix·er
mix·ture
moan
mo·bile
mo·bil·i·ty
mo·bi·lize
moc·ca·sin
mock
mock·er·y
mode
mod·el
mod·er·ate
mod·er·a·tion

mod·ern
mod·ern·ize
mod·est
mod·es·ty
mod·i·fi·ca·tion
mod·i·fy
mod·u·late
moist
moist·en
mois·ture
mo·lar
mo·las·ses
mold
mold·ing
mold·y
mole
mo·lec·u·lar
mol·e·cule
mo·lest
mol·ten
mo·ment
mo·men·tar·y
mo·men·tum
mon·arch
mon·ar·chy
mon·as·ter·y
mon·e·tar·y
mon·ey
mon·grel
mon·i·tor
monk
mon·key
mon·o·gram
mon·o·logue
mo·nop·o·lize
mo·nop·o·ly
mo·not·o·nous
mon·ster
mon·strous
month
mon·u·ment
mon·u·men·tal
mood
moon

moon·light
moon·shine
moose
mope
mor·al
mo·rale
mo·ral·i·ty
mor·al·ize
mor·bid
more·o·ver
morgue
morn·ing
mo·ron
mor·phine
mor·sel
mor·tal
mor·tal·i·ty
mor·tar
mort·gage
mor·ti·fy
mor·tu·ar·y
mo·sa·ic
mos·qui·to
moss
mo·tel
moth
moth·er
mo·tif
mo·tion
mo·ti·vate
mo·tive
mot·ley
mo·tor
mo·tor·cy·cle
mo·tor·ist
mo·tor·man
mot·tle
mot·to
mound
mount
moun·tain
moun·tain·eer
moun·tain·ous
mourn

mourn·er
mourn·ful
mouse
mouth
mouth·ful
mov·a·ble
move
move·ment
mov·er
mov·ie
mov·ing
mow
mow·er
mud·dle
mud·dy
muff
muf·fin
muf·fle
muf·fler
mug·ger
mule
mul·ti·col·ored
mul·ti·lat·er·al
mul·ti·ple
mul·ti·pli·ca·tion
mul·ti·plic·i·ty
mul·ti·pli·er
mul·ti·ply
mul·ti·tude
mum·ble
munch
mu·nic·i·pal
mu·ni·tions
mu·ral
mur·der
mur·der·er
mur·der·ous
murk·y
mur·mur
mus·cle
mus·cu·lar
muse
mu·se·um
mush

mush·room
mu·sic
mu·si·cal
mu·si·cian
mu·si·col·o·gy
musk
mus·ket
musk·rat
mus·lin
mus·tache
mus·tard
mus·ter
mu·ta·tion
mute
mu·ti·late
mu·ti·ny
mut·ter
mu·tu·al
muz·zle
myr·i·ad
mys·te·ri·ous
mys·ter·y
mys·ti·cal
mys·ti·cism
myth
myth·i·cal
my·thol·o·gy

N

nail
na·ive
na·ked
name·less
name·ly
nap·kin
nar·cot·ic
nar·rate
nar·ra·tive
nar·row
nar·row-mind·ed
na·sal
nas·ty

na·tion
na·tion·al
na·tion·al·i·ty
na·tion·al·ize
na·tive
na·tiv·i·ty
nat·u·ral
nat·u·ral·ize
na·ture
naugh·ty
nau·sea
nau·seous
nau·ti·cal
na·val
nave
na·vel
nav·i·ga·ble
nav·i·gate
nav·i·ga·tion
nav·i·ga·tor
na·vy
near·by
neat
nec·es·sar·y
ne·ces·si·ty
neck·lace
neck·line
nec·tar
need
nee·dle
nee·dle·point
need·y
ne·gate
neg·a·tive
neg·lect
neg·li·gence
neg·li·gent
neg·li·gi·ble
ne·go·tia·ble
ne·go·ti·ate
ne·go·ti·a·tion
Ne·gro
neigh·bor
neigh·bor·hood

nei·ther
ne·on
neph·ew
nerve
nerv·ous
nest
nes·tle
neth·er
net·work
neu·rol·o·gy
neu·ro·sis
neu·rot·ic
neu·ter
neu·tral
neu·tral·i·ty
neu·tral·ize
neu·tron
nev·er
nev·er·the·less
new·born
new·com·er
news
news·cast
news·let·ter
news·pa·per
news·print
news·reel
news·stand
next
nib·ble
nice
nick
nick·el
nick·name
nic·o·tine
niece
night
night·cap
night·fall
night·gown
night·ly
night·mare
night school
night·time

nim·ble
nine
nine·teen
nine·teenth
nine·ti·eth
nine·ty
ninth
nip·ple
ni·tro·gen
ni·tro·glyc·er·in
no·bil·i·ty
no·ble
no·bly
no·bod·y
noc·tur·nal
noise
nois·y
no·mad
no·men·cla·ture
nom·i·nal
nom·i·nate
nom·i·na·tion
nom·i·nee
non·ag·gres·sion
non·com·mis·sioned
non·com·mit·tal
non·con·form·ist
none
non·en·ti·ty
non·ex·ist·ent
non·par·ti·san
non·prof·it
non·res·i·dent
non·sec·tar·i·an
non·sense
non·stop
non·vi·o·lent
noon
noon·day
noon·time
nor
nor·mal
nor·mal·ize
north

north·east
north·east·ern
north·ern
north·ern·most
north·ward
north·west
north·west·ern
nose
nos·tal·gia
nos·tril
no·ta·ble
no·ta·rize
no·ta·ry pub·lic
no·ta·tion
notch
note
note·book
note·wor·thy
noth·ing
no·tice
no·tice·a·ble
no·ti·fi·ca·tion
no·ti·fy
no·tion
no·to·ri·e·ty
no·to·ri·ous
not·with·stand·ing
noun
nour·ish
no·va
nov·el
nov·el·ty
nov·ice
now·a·days
no·where
nox·ious
noz·zle
nu·cle·ar
nu·cle·us
nude
nug·get
nui·sance
nul·li·fi·ca·tion
nul·li·fy

numb
num·ber
nu·mer·al
nu·mer·i·cal
nu·mer·ous
nup·tial
nurse
nurs·er·y
nur·ture
nut·meg
nu·tri·ent
nu·tri·tion
nu·tri·tious
nut·shell
nut·ty
nuz·zle

O

oak
oar
o·a·sis
oat
oath
o·be·di·ence
o·be·di·ent
o·bese
o·bey
o·bit·u·ar·y
ob·ject
ob·jec·tion
ob·jec·tive
ob·li·ga·tion
o·blige
ob·lique
ob·lit·er·ate
ob·liv·i·on
ob·nox·ious
ob·scene
ob·scen·i·ty
ob·scure
ob·scu·ri·ty
ob·se·qui·ous
ob·serv·ance

ob·serv·ant
ob·ser·va·tion
ob·serv·a·to·ry
ob·serve
ob·sess
ob·ses·sion
ob·so·les·cence
ob·so·les·cent
ob·so·lete
ob·sta·cle
ob·ste·tri·cian
ob·stet·rics
ob·sti·na·cy
ob·sti·nate
ob·struct
ob·struc·tion
ob·tain
ob·tain·a·ble
ob·tru·sive
ob·tuse
ob·vi·ous
oc·ca·sion
oc·ca·sion·al
oc·cult
oc·cu·pant
oc·cu·pa·tion
oc·cu·py
oc·cur
oc·cur·rence
o·cean
o'clock
oc·tave
odd
ode
o·di·ous
o·dom·e·ter
o·dor
off·beat
of·fend
of·fend·er
of·fense
of·fen·sive
of·fer
off·hand

of·fice
of·fi·cer
of·fi·cial
of·fi·ci·ate
of·fi·cious
off·set
off·shoot
off·shore
off·spring
off-the-rec·ord
of·ten
o·gre
oil
oil·y
oint·ment
old-fash·ioned
ol·ive
om·e·let
o·men
om·i·nous
o·mis·sion
o·mit
om·nip·o·tent
once
on·com·ing
one·self
one-sid·ed
on·go·ing
on·ion
on·look·er
on·ly
on·rush
on·set
on·shore
on·slaught
on·ward
ooze
o·paque
o·pen
o·pen·ing
o·pen-mind·ed
op·er·a
op·er·ate
op·er·a·tion

77

op·er·a·tor
oph·thal·mol·o·gy
o·pin·ion
o·pin·ion·at·ed
o·pi·um
o·pos·sum
op·po·nent
op·por·tun·ist
op·por·tu·ni·ty
op·pose
op·po·site
op·po·si·tion
op·press
op·pres·sive
op·tic
op·ti·cal
op·ti·cian
op·ti·mism
op·ti·mis·tic
op·tion
op·tom·e·trist
op·u·lence
o·ra·cle
o·ral
or·ange
o·ra·tion
or·a·tor
or·a·to·ry
or·bit
or·chard
or·ches·tra
or·chid
or·dain
or·deal
or·der
or·di·nance
or·di·nar·i·ly
or·di·nar·y
ord·nance
ore
or·gan
or·gan·ic
or·gan·ism
or·gan·i·za·tion

or·gan·ize
o·ri·ent
O·ri·en·tal
o·ri·en·ta·tion
o·ri·gin
o·rig·i·nal
o·rig·i·nate
o·rig·i·na·tor
or·na·ment
or·nate
or·phan
or·tho·don·tia
or·tho·dox
or·tho·dox·y
or·tho·pe·dics
os·cil·late
os·mo·sis
os·si·fy
os·ten·si·bly
os·ten·ta·tious
os·tra·cize
os·trich
oth·er·wise
ought
ounce
our·self
our·selves
oust
out·break
out·cast
out·come
out·cry
out·dis·tance
out·doors
out·er
out·fit
out·go·ing
out·grow
out·ing
out·land·ish
out·law
out·let
out·line
out·live

out·look
out·ly·ing
out·num·ber
out-of-date
out·post
out·put
out·ra·geous
out·right
out·run
out·side
out·skirts
out·spo·ken
out·stand·ing
out·strip
out·ward
out·wit
o·val
o·va·ry
o·va·tion
ov·en
o·ver·alls
o·ver·bear·ing
o·ver·board
o·ver·cast
o·ver·coat
o·ver·come
o·ver·flow
o·ver·grown
o·ver·head
o·ver·heard
o·ver·land
o·ver·lap
o·ver·load
o·ver·look
o·ver·night
o·ver·pass
o·ver·pow·er
o·ver·rule
o·ver·run
o·ver·seas
o·ver·se·er
o·ver·shad·ow
o·ver·shoe
o·ver·sight

o·ver·step
o·vert
o·ver·take
o·ver·throw
o·ver·time
o·ver·tone
o·ver·ture
o·ver·turn
o·ver·weight
o·ver·whelm
o·ver·work
owe
owl
own·er
own·er·ship
ox
ox·y·gen
oys·ter
o·zone

P

pace
pa·cif·ic
pac·i·fy
pack
pack·age
pack·er
pact
pad·dle
pad·lock
pa·gan
page
pag·eant
paid
pail
pain
paint
paint·er
pair
pa·ja·mas
pal·ace
pal·at·a·ble
pal·ate

pa·la·tial	par·don
pale	pare
pal·ette	par·ent
palm	pa·ren·tal
pal·pa·ble	pa·ren·the·sis
pal·pi·tate	par·ish
pal·sy	par·ish·ion·er
pal·try	par·i·ty
pam·per	park
pam·phlet	par·ley
pan·a·ce·a	par·lia·ment
pan·cake	par·lia·men·ta·ry
pane	par·lor
pan·el	pa·ro·chi·al
pan·el·ing	par·o·dy
pang	pa·role
pan·ic	par·ry
pan·ick·y	pars·ley
pan·o·ply	part
pan·o·ram·a	par·take
pan·sy	par·tial
pant	par·ti·al·i·ty
pan·to·mime	par·tic·i·pate
pan·try	par·ti·cle
pants	par·tic·u·lar
pa·pal	par·ti·san
pa·per	par·ti·tion
pa·per·back	part·ner·ship
par·a·ble	part-time
par·a·chute	par·ty
pa·rade	pass
par·a·dise	pas·sage
par·a·dox	pas·sage·way
par·af·fin	pas·sen·ger
par·a·graph	pas·sion
par·al·lel	pas·sion·ate
pa·ral·y·sis	pas·sive
par·a·lyze	pass·port
par·a·mount	past
par·a·phrase	paste
par·a·site	pas·tel
par·a·troop·er	pas·teur·ize
par·cel	pas·time
parch	pas·tor·al

pas·try

pas·ture

patch

pat·ent

pa·ter·nal

path

pa·thet·ic

path·way

pa·tience

pa·tient

pat·i·o

pa·tri·arch

pa·tri·ot

pa·tri·ot·ic

pa·trol

pa·trol·man

pa·tron

pa·tron·age

pa·tron·ize

pat·tern

pat·ty

pause

pave·ment

pa·vil·ion

paw

pawn

pay

pay·a·ble

pay·ment

pay·roll

pea

peace

peace·ful

peach

pea·cock

peak

pea·nut

pear

pearl

peas·ant

peb·ble

pe·can

peck

pe·cul·iar

pe·cu·li·ar·i·ty

ped·al

pe·dan·tic

ped·ant·ry

ped·dle

ped·dler

ped·es·tal

pe·des·tri·an

pe·di·a·tri·cian

ped·i·gree

peek

peel

peep

peer

pee·vish

pel·i·can

pel·let

pelt

pel·vic

pe·nal·ize

pen·al·ty

pen·ance

pen·cil

pend·ing

pen·du·lum

pen·e·tra·ble

pen·e·trate

pen·e·trat·ing

pen·guin

pen·i·cil·lin

pe·nin·su·la

pen·i·tent

pen·i·ten·tia·ry

pen·knife

pen·nant

pen·ni·less

pen·ny

pen·sion

pen·ta·gon

peo·ple

pep·per

per·cale

per·ceive

per cent

per·cent·age
per·cep·ti·ble
per·cep·tion
perch
per·co·late
per·cus·sion
per·en·ni·al
per·fect
per·fec·tion
per·fo·rate
per·form
per·form·ance
per·fume
per·haps
per·il
per·il·ous
pe·rim·e·ter
pe·ri·od
pe·ri·od·i·cal
pe·riph·er·al
per·ish
per·jure
per·ju·ry
per·ma·nent
per·me·a·ble
per·me·ate
per·mis·sion
per·mit
per·ni·cious
per·pe·trate
per·pe·tra·tor
per·pet·u·al
per·pet·u·ate
per·pe·tu·i·ty
per·plex
per·plex·i·ty
per·se·cute
per·se·cu·tion
per·se·cu·tor
per·se·ver·ance
per·se·vere
per·sist
per·sist·ence
per·sist·ent

per·son
per·son·a·ble
per·son·al
per·son·al·i·ty
per·son·i·fy
per·spec·tive
per·spi·ra·tion
per·suade
per·sua·sion
per·sua·sive
per·tain
per·ti·nence
per·ti·nent
pe·ruse
per·vade
per·verse
per·ver·sion
per·vert
pes·si·mism
pes·si·mis·tic
pet·al
pe·ti·tion
pe·tro·le·um
pet·ty
pet·u·lant
pew·ter
phan·tom
phar·ma·ceu·ti·cal
phar·ma·cist
phase
pheas·ant
phe·nom·e·nal
phe·nom·e·non
phil·an·throp·ic
phi·lan·thro·pist
phil·har·mon·ic
phi·los·o·pher
phil·o·soph·i·cal
phi·los·o·phy
phlegm
pho·bi·a
phoe·nix
phone
pho·net·ic

pho·no·graph
phos·phate
phos·phor·ous
phos·phor·us
pho·to
pho·to·graph
pho·tog·ra·pher
pho·to·graph·ic
phrase
phys·i·cal
phy·si·cian
phys·i·cist
phys·ics
phys·i·ol·o·gy
pi·an·ist
pi·an·o
pick
pick·er
pick·et
pick·le
pic·nic
pic·ture
pic·tur·esque
pie
piece
piece·meal
pier
pierce
pi·e·ty
pi·geon
pig·gy
pig·ment
pike
pile
pil·fer
pil·grim
pil·grim·age
pill
pil·lage
pil·lar
pil·low
pi·lot
pi·lot light
pim·ple

pin·cers
pinch
pine
pine·ap·ple
pink
pin·na·cle
pin·point
pint
pi·o·neer
pi·ous
pipe
pipe·line
pip·er
pique
pi·ra·cy
pi·rate
pis·tol
pis·ton
pitch
pitch·er
pit·fall
pith
pit·i·a·ble
pit·i·ful
pit·i·less
pit·y
piv·ot
piz·za
pla·ca·ble
pla·cate
place
plac·id
plague
plaid
plain
plan
plane
plan·et
plank
plant
plan·ta·tion
plant·er
plas·ma
plas·ter

plas·tic
plate
pla·teau
plat·form
plat·i·num
plat·i·tude
pla·toon
plat·ter
plau·si·ble
play
play·er
play·ful
play·ground
play·mate
play-off
plea
plead
pleas·ant
pleas·ant·ry
please
pleas·ure
pleat
pledge
ple·na·ry
plen·ti·ful
plen·ty
pli·a·ble
pli·ant
pli·ers
plight
plod
plot
plow
plow·share
pluck
plug
plum
plum·age
plumb·er
plume
plum·met
plump
plun·der
plunge

plur·al
plu·ral·i·ty
plus
plush
plu·to·ni·um
ply
ply·wood
pneu·mat·ic
pneu·mo·nia
pock·et
pock·et·book
po·em
po·et
po·et·ic
po·et·ry
point
point-blank
poise
poi·son
poi·son·ous
poke
pok·er
po·lar
po·lar·i·ty
pole
po·lem·ic
po·lice
po·lice·man
po·lice·wom·an
pol·i·cy
po·li·o
pol·ish
po·lite
pol·i·tic
po·lit·i·cal
pol·i·ti·cian
pol·i·tics
pol·ka
poll
pol·len
pol·li·nate
pol·lute
pol·lu·tion
po·lo

po·lyg·a·my
pol·yp
pomp
pom·pous
pond
pon·der
pon·tiff
po·ny
poo·dle
pool
poor
pope
pop·lar
pop·lin
pop·py
pop·u·lace
pop·u·lar
pop·u·lar·i·ty
pop·u·lar·i·za·tion
pop·u·la·tion
pop·u·lous
por·ce·lain
porch
pore
pork
po·rous
por·poise
por·ridge
port
port·a·ble
por·tend
por·tent
por·ten·tous
por·ter
port·hole
por·tion
por·trait
por·tray
pose
po·si·tion
pos·i·tive
pos·sess
pos·ses·sion
pos·ses·sive

pos·ses·sor
pos·si·bil·i·ty
pos·si·ble
pos·si·bly
pos·sum
post
post·age
post·al
post card
pos·te·ri·or
pos·ter·i·ty
post·man
post·mark
post·mas·ter
post of·fice
post·pone
post·script
pos·tu·late
pos·ture
po·tas·si·um
po·ta·to
po·ten·cy
po·tent
po·ten·tate
po·ten·tial
po·ten·ti·al·i·ty
pot·hole
po·tion
pot·pour·ri
pot·ter
pouch
poul·try
pounce
pound
pour
pov·er·ty
pow·der
pow·er
pow·er·ful
prac·ti·cal
prac·ti·cal·i·ty
prac·tice
prac·ti·tion·er
prag·mat·ic

prai·rie
praise
prank
pray
prayer
preach
preach·er
pre·am·ble
pre·car·i·ous
pre·cau·tion
pre·cede
prec·e·dent
pre·cept
pre·cinct
pre·cious
pre·cip·i·tate
pre·cip·i·ta·tion
pre·cise
pre·ci·sion
pre·co·cious
pred·a·to·ry
pred·e·ces·sor
pre·de·ter·mine
pre·dic·a·ment
pred·i·cate
pre·dict
pre·dic·tion
pre·di·lec·tion
pre·dis·po·si·tion
pre·dom·i·nant
pre·dom·i·nate
pre·em·i·nent
pre·empt
pre·fab·ri·cate
pref·ace
pre·fer
pref·er·ence
pref·e·ren·tial
pre·fix
preg·nan·cy
preg·nant
pre·his·to·ric
prej·u·dice
prel·ate

pre·lim·i·nar·y
prel·ude
pre·ma·ture
pre·med·i·tate
pre·mier
prem·ise
pre·mi·um
pre·paid
prep·a·ra·tion
pre·par·a·to·ry
pre·pare
pre·pon·der·ance
prep·o·si·tion
pre·pos·sess·ing
pre·pos·ter·ous
pre·req·ui·site
pre·rog·a·tive
Pres·by·te·ri·an
pre·school
pre·sci·ence
pre·scribe
pre·scrip·tion
pres·ence
pres·ent
pre·sent·a·ble
pres·en·ta·tion
pres·er·va·tion
pre·serv·a·tive
pre·serve
pre·serv·er
pre·side
pres·i·den·cy
pres·i·dent
pres·i·den·tial
press
pres·sure
pres·sur·ize
pres·tige
pre·sume
pre·sump·tion
pre·sump·tu·ous
pre·tend
pre·tense
pre·ten·sion

pre·ten·tious
pre·text
pret·ty
pre·vail
prev·a·lent
pre·vent
pre·ven·tion
pre·view
pre·vi·ous
prey
price
prick
prick·le
pride
priest
pri·ma·ry
pri·mate
prime
prim·er
prim·i·tive
prim·rose
prince
prin·cess
prin·ci·pal
prin·ci·pal·i·ty
prin·ci·pal·ly
prin·ci·ple
print
print·er
pri·or
pri·or·i·ty
prism
pris·on
pris·on·er
pri·va·cy
pri·vate
priv·i·lege
prize
prob·a·bil·i·ty
prob·a·ble
pro·ba·tion
probe
prob·lem
pro·ce·dure

pro·ceed
proc·ess
pro·ces·sion
proc·es·sor
pro·claim
proc·la·ma·tion
pro·cure
prod·i·gal
pro·di·gious
prod·i·gy
pro·duce
prod·uct
pro·duc·tion
pro·fane
pro·fess
pro·fes·sion
pro·fes·sion·al
pro·fes·sor
pro·fi·cient
pro·file
prof·it
prof·it·a·ble
pro·found
pro·fuse
pro·gram
prog·ress
pro·gres·sive
pro·hib·it
pro·hi·bi·tion
pro·hib·i·tive
proj·ect
pro·jec·tion
pro·lif·ic
pro·logue
pro·long
prom·e·nade
prom·i·nence
prom·i·nent
prom·ise
prom·is·so·ry
prom·on·to·ry
pro·mote
pro·mo·tion
prompt

prone
pro·noun
pro·nounce
pro·nun·ci·a·tion
proof
prop
prop·a·gan·da
prop·a·gate
pro·pen·si·ty
prop·er
prop·er·ty
proph·e·cy
proph·e·sy
proph·et
pro·phet·ic
pro·pi·tious
pro·por·tion
pro·pos·al
pro·pose
prop·o·si·tion
pro·pri·e·tor
pro·pri·e·ty
pro·pul·sion
pro·sa·ic
prose
pros·e·cute
pros·e·cu·tion
pros·e·cu·tor
pros·pect
pro·spec·tive
pros·per
pros·per·i·ty
pros·per·ous
pros·the·sis
pros·ti·tute
pros·trate
pro·tect
pro·tec·tion
pro·tec·tive
pro·tec·tor
pro·test
Prot·es·tant
pro·ton
pro·to·type

pro·trude
pro·tru·sion
proud
prove
prov·erb
pro·vide
prov·i·dence
prov·ince
pro·vin·cial
pro·vi·sion
prov·o·ca·tion
pro·voke
prow·ess
prowl
prox·im·i·ty
prox·y
prude
pru·dence
pru·dent
prune
pry
psalm
pseu·do
psy·chi·at·ric
psy·chi·a·trist
psy·chi·a·try
psy·chic
psy·cho·a·nal·y·sis
psy·cho·an·a·lyst
psy·cho·log·i·cal·ly
psy·chol·o·gist
psy·chol·o·gy
psy·cho·sis
psy·cho·ther·a·py
psy·chot·ic
pu·ber·ty
pub·lic
pub·li·ca·tion
pub·lic·i·ty
pub·lish
pub·lish·er
pud·ding
pud·dle
puff

pulp
pul·pit
pul·sate
pulse
pul·ve·rize
pump
pump·kin
punch
punc·tu·al
punc·tu·ate
punc·tu·a·tion
pun·gent
pun·ish
pun·ish·ment
pu·ny
pu·pil
pup·pet
pup·py
pur·chase
pur·chas·er
pure
purge
pur·i·fi·ca·tion
pu·ri·fy
pu·ri·ty
pur·ple
pur·port
pur·pose
purse
pur·su·ant
pur·sue
pur·su·er
pur·suit
pus
push
pu·trid
put·ty
puz·zle
pyr·a·mid
py·thon

quake
qual·i·fi·ca·tion
qual·i·fied
qual·i·fy
qual·i·ta·tive
qual·i·ty
qualm
quan·ti·ta·tive
quan·ti·ty
quar·an·tine
quar·rel
quar·ry
quart
quar·ter
quar·ter·back
quar·tet
quartz
queen
queer
que·ry
quest
ques·tion
ques·tion·naire
quib·ble
quick
quick·en
qui·et
quilt
qui·nine
quin·tet
quirk
quit
quite
quiv·er
quiz
quo·rum
quo·ta
quo·ta·tion
quote
quo·tient

Q

quack

R

rab·bi

rab·bit
rab·id
ra·bies
rac·coon
race
rac·er
rac·ism
rack
rack·et
ra·dar
ra·di·al
ra·di·ant
ra·di·ate
ra·di·a·tion
ra·di·a·tor
rad·i·cal
ra·di·o
ra·di·o·ac·tive
ra·di·o·ac·tiv·i·ty
ra·di·ol·o·gy
ra·di·um
ra·di·us
raf·fle
raft
rage
rag·ged
rag·time
raid
rail
rail·road
rain
rain·bow
rain·coat
rain·fall
rain·storm
rain·y
raise
rai·sin
rake
ral·ly
ram·ble
ram·i·fi·ca·tion
ram·page
ramp·ant

ranch
ran·cid
ran·cor
ran·dom
rang
range
rang·er
rank
ran·sack
ran·som
rap
rape
rap·id
rap·port
rapt
rap·ture
rare
rar·i·ty
ras·cal
rash
rasp·ber·ry
rate
rath·er
rat·i·fy
ra·ti·o
ra·tion
ra·tion·al
rat·tle
rav·age
rave
rav·el
ra·ven
rav·en·ous
rav·ish
ray·on
ra·zor
reach
re·act
re·ac·tion
re·ac·tor
read
read·i·ly
read·i·ness
re·ad·just·ment

read·y
re·al
re·al·ism
re·al·is·tic
re·al·i·ty
re·al·ize
re·al·ly
realm
reap
re·ap·pear
rear
re·ar·range
rea·son
rea·son·a·ble
re·as·sem·ble
re·as·sure
reb·el
re·bel·lion
re·bel·lious
re·bound
re·buff
re·build
re·buke
re·call
re·cap·ture
re·cede
re·ceipt
re·ceive
re·ceiv·er
re·cent
re·cep·ta·cle
re·cep·tion
re·cess
re·ces·sion
rec·i·pe
re·cip·i·ent
re·cip·ro·cal
re·cip·ro·cate
re·cit·al
rec·i·ta·tion
re·cite
reck·less
re·claim
re·cline

rec·og·ni·tion
re·cog·ni·zance
rec·og·nize
rec·ol·lect
rec·om·mend
rec·om·men·da·tion
rec·om·pense
rec·on·cile
rec·on·cil·i·a·tion
re·con·sid·er
re·cord
re·cord·er
re·count
re·course
re·cov·er
re·cov·er·y
rec·re·a·tion
re·crim·i·na·tion
re·cruit
rec·tan·gle
rec·tan·gu·lar
rec·ti·fy
rec·tor
re·cu·per·ate
re·cur
re·cur·rence
re·deem
re·demp·tion
re·dou·ble
re·dress
re·duce
re·duc·i·ble
re·duc·tion
re·dun·dant
reed
reef
reek
reel
re·e·lect
re·e·lec·tion
re·en·ter
re·en·try
re·es·tab·lish
re·fer

ref·e·ree
ref·er·ence
ref·er·en·dum
re·fill
re·fine
re·fine·ment
re·fin·er·y
re·flect
re·flec·tion
re·flex
re·form
ref·or·ma·tion
re·fract
re·frain
re·fresh·er
re·fresh·ment
re·frig·er·a·tor
ref·uge
ref·u·gee
re·fund
re·fus·al
re·fuse
re·fute
re·gain
re·gard
re·gard·ing
re·gard·less
re·gen·er·ate
re·gent
re·gime
reg·i·men
reg·i·ment
re·gion
reg·is·ter
reg·is·tra·tion
re·gres·sion
re·gret
re·gret·ta·ble
reg·u·lar
reg·u·late
reg·u·la·tion
reg·u·la·tor
reg·u·la·to·ry
re·ha·bil·i·tate

re·hash
re·hears·al
re·hearse
reign
re·im·burse
re·in·force
re·in·state
re·it·er·ate
re·ject
re·joice
re·ju·ve·nate
re·lapse
re·late
re·la·tion
rel·a·tive
rel·a·tiv·i·ty
re·lax
re·lay
re·lease
re·lent
rel·e·van·cy
re·li·a·bil·i·ty
re·li·a·ble
re·li·ance
rel·ic
re·lief
re·lieve
re·li·gion
re·li·gious
re·lin·quish
rel·ish
re·luc·tance
re·luc·tant
re·ly
re·main
re·main·der
re·mark
re·mark·a·ble
re·me·di·al
rem·e·dy
re·mem·ber
re·mem·brance
re·mind
re·mind·er

rem·i·nis·cent
re·mis·sion
re·mit
re·mit·tance
rem·nant
re·morse
re·mote
re·mov·al
re·move
re·mov·er
re·mu·ner·ate
ren·der
re·new
re·new·a·ble
re·new·al
re·nounce
ren·o·vate
rent
rent·al
re·nun·ci·a·tion
re·o·pen
re·or·gan·ize
re·pair
re·pair·man
rep·a·ra·tion
re·past
re·pay
re·peal
re·peat
re·pel
re·pel·lent
re·pent
re·pent·ance
re·per·cus·sion
rep·er·toire
rep·e·ti·tion
rep·e·ti·tious
re·place
re·plen·ish
rep·li·ca
re·ply
re·port
re·pose
rep·re·hen·si·ble

rep·re·sent
rep·re·sen·ta·tion
rep·re·sent·a·tive
re·press
re·pres·sion
re·prieve
rep·ri·mand
re·proach
re·pro·duce
re·pro·duc·tion
rep·tile
re·pub·lic
re·pub·li·can
re·pu·di·ate
re·pug·nant
re·pulse
re·pul·sive
rep·u·ta·ble
rep·u·ta·tion
re·quest
re·quire
re·quire·ment
req·ui·site
req·ui·si·tion
re·scind
res·cue
re·search
re·sem·blance
re·sem·ble
re·sent
re·sent·ment
res·er·va·tion
re·serve
res·er·voir
re·side
res·i·dence
res·i·dent
re·sid·u·al
res·i·due
re·sign
res·ig·na·tion
re·sil·i·ent
res·in
re·sist

re·sist·ance
res·o·lu·tion
re·solve
re·sort
re·sound
re·source
re·spect
re·spect·a·ble
re·spect·ful
re·spec·tive
res·pi·ra·tion
res·pi·ra·tor
res·pite
re·spond
re·sponse
re·spon·si·bil·i·ty
re·spon·si·ble
rest
res·tau·rant
rest·ful
res·ti·tu·tion
rest·less
res·to·ra·tion
re·store
re·strain
re·straint
re·strict
re·stric·tion
rest room
re·sult
re·sume
re·sump·tion
re·sus·ci·ta·tor
re·tail
re·tain
re·tain·er
re·tal·i·ate
re·tard·ed
re·ten·tion
ret·i·cent
ret·i·na
re·tire
re·tire·ment
re·tort

re·touch
re·trace
re·tract
re·tread
re·treat
ret·ri·bu·tion
re·trieve
ret·ro·ac·tive
ret·ro·gres·sion
ret·ro·spect
re·turn
re·un·ion
re·u·nite
re·veal
rev·el
rev·e·la·tion
re·venge
rev·e·nue
re·vere
rev·er·ence
Rev·er·end
rev·er·ent
re·verse
re·vers·i·ble
re·vert
re·view
re·viv·al
re·vive
re·volt
rev·o·lu·tion
rev·o·lu·tion·ar·y
rev·o·lu·tion·ize
re·volve
re·volv·er
re·vue
re·vul·sion
re·ward
rhap·so·dy
rhet·o·ric
rheu·ma·tism
rhi·noc·er·os
rhyme
rhythm
rhyth·mi·cal

rib·bon	roar
rice	roast
rich	rob·ber
rich·es	rob·ber·y
rid	robe
rid·den	rob·in
rid·dle	ro·bot
ride	ro·bust
rid·er	rock
ridge	rock·er
rid·i·cule	rock·et
ri·dic·u·lous	rock·y
ri·fle	rode
rift	ro·dent
right	role
right·eous	roll
right-hand	roll·er
rig·id	ro·mance
rig·or	ro·man·tic
rig·or·ous	ro·man·ti·cize
rind	romp
ring	roof
ring·er	roof·ing
rinse	room
ri·ot	room·y
ri·ot·ous	roost
ripe	roost·er
rip·en	root
rip·ple	rope
rise	ro·sa·ry
ris·en	rose
risk	ro·sette
rit·u·al	ros·y
ri·val	ro·ta·ry
riv·er	ro·tate
riv·er·side	ro·tor
riv·et	rot·ten
roach	ro·tun·da
road	rough
road·block	round
road map	round·up
road·side	rouse
road·way	route
roam	rou·tine

rove
row
row·dy
roy·al
roy·al·ty
rub·ber
rub·bish
rub·ble
ru·by
rud·der
rude
ru·di·men·ta·ry
ruf·fle
rug·ged
ru·in
ru·in·ous
rule
rul·er
rum·ble
rum·mage
ru·mor
rump
run·a·way
run·down
rung
run·ner
run·off
run·way
rup·ture
ru·ral
ruse
rush
rust
rus·tic
rus·tler
rust·y
ruth·less

S

Sab·bath
sa·ber
sab·o·tage
sac·cha·rin

sa·chet
sack
sac·ra·ment
sa·cred
sac·ri·fice
sad·den
sad·dle
sa·dist
safe
safe·guard
safe·keep·ing
safe·ty
sage
sail
sail·boat
sail·or
saint
sake
sal·ad
sal·a·ry
sale
sales·clerk
sales·man
sa·li·ent
sa·line
sa·li·va
sal·ly
salm·on
sa·loon
salt
salt·wa·ter
sal·u·tar·y
sal·u·ta·tion
sa·lute
sal·vage
sal·va·tion
sam·ple
sanc·ti·fy
sanc·tion
sanc·ti·ty
sanc·tu·ar·y
sand
san·dal
sand·blast

sand·box
sand·pa·per
sand·stone
sand·wich
sane
sang
san·i·tar·y
san·i·ta·tion
san·i·ty
sank
sap·phire
sar·casm
sar·cas·tic
sar·dine
sash
Sa·tan
sa·teen
sat·el·lite
sa·ti·ate
sat·in
sat·ire
sat·i·rize
sat·is·fac·tion
sat·is·fac·to·ry
sat·is·fy
sat·u·rate
sat·u·ra·tion
sauce
sauce·pan
sau·cer
sau·cy
sauer·kraut
sau·sage
sav·age
save
sav·er
sav·ior
sa·vor·y
saw·dust
saw·mill
sax·o·phone
scab
scaf·fold
scald

scale
scal·lop
scalp
scal·y
scam·per
scan
scan·dal
scant
scant·y
scape·goat
scar
scarce
scar·ci·ty
scare
scare·crow
scarf
scar·let
scat·ter
scav·en·ger
scene
scen·er·y
sce·nic
scent
scep·ter
sched·ule
scheme
schism
schol·ar
schol·ar·ship
scho·las·tic
school
school·book
school·chil·dren
school·room
school·teach·er
school·work
school year
sci·ence
sci·en·tif·ic
sci·en·tist
scis·sors
scoff
scold
scoop

scope
scorch
score
score·board
scorn
scor·pi·on
scoun·drel
scour
scourge
scout
scowl
scram·ble
scrap
scrape
scrap·er
scratch
scrawl
scream
screech
screen
screw
screw·driv·er
scrib·ble
script
Scrip·ture
scroll
scrub
scru·ple
scru·pu·lous
scru·ti·nize
scru·ti·ny
scuf·fle
sculp·tor
sculp·ture
scum
scur·ry
scut·tle
sea
sea·board
sea·coast
sea·far·ing
sea·food
sea gull
seal

seam
sea·man
seam·stress
sé·ance
sea·port
sear
search
sea·shore
sea·sick
sea·side
sea·son
sea·son·a·ble
seat
sea·wa·ter
sea·wor·thy
se·cede
se·ces·sion
se·clude
se·clu·sion
sec·ond
sec·ond·ar·y
se·cre·cy
se·cret
sec·re·tar·i·al
sec·re·tar·y
se·crete
se·cre·tion
sect
sec·tion
sec·u·lar
se·cure
se·cu·ri·ty
se·dan
se·date
sed·a·tive
sed·i·ment
se·di·tion
se·duce
se·duc·tive
see
seed
seek
seem
seem·ly

seen
seg·ment
seg·re·ga·tion
seis·mic
seize
sei·zure
sel·dom
se·lect
se·lec·tion
self
self-as·sur·ance
self-cen·tered
self-con·fi·dence
self-con·scious
self-de·fense
self-em·ployed
self-ev·i·dent
self-help
self-im·prove·ment
self-in·dul·gent
self·ish
self·less
self-pres·er·va·tion
self-re·li·ant
self-right·eous
self-sac·ri·fice
self-sat·is·fied
self-serv·ice
self-suf·fi·cient
self-wind·ing
sell
sell·er
selves
sem·blance
se·mes·ter
sem·i·au·to·mat·ic
sem·i·cir·cle
sem·i·cir·cu·lar
sem·i·con·duc·tor
sem·i·fi·nal
sem·i·nar
sem·i·nar·y
sen·ate
sen·a·tor

send
se·nile
sen·ior
sen·sa·tion
sen·sa·tion·al
sense
sen·si·bil·i·ty
sen·si·ble
sen·si·tive
sen·su·al
sen·su·ous
sent
sen·tence
sen·ti·ment
sen·ti·nel
sen·try
sep·a·rate
sep·a·ra·tion
se·quel
se·quence
se·ques·ter
ser·e·nade
se·rene
ser·geant
se·ri·al
se·ries
se·ri·ous
ser·mon
ser·pent
se·rum
serv·ant
serve
serv·er
serv·ice
serv·ice·a·ble
ser·vile
ser·vi·tude
ses·a·me
ses·sion
set·tle
set·tle·ment
set·tler
sev·en
sev·en·teen

sev·enth	sheen
sev·en·ti·eth	sheep
sev·en·ty	sheep·ish
sev·er	sheep·skin
sev·er·al	sheer
sev·er·ance	sheet
se·vere	shelf
se·ver·i·ty	shell
sew	shel·lac
sew·age	shell·fish
sew·er	shel·ter
sex	shelve
sex·ton	shep·herd
sex·u·al	sher·bet
shab·by	sher·iff
shack	sher·ry
shack·le	shield
shade	shift
shad·ow	shil·ling
shad·y	shim·mer
shaft	shin
shag·gy	shine
shake	shin·gle
shak·er	shin·y
shake·up	ship
shak·y	ship·build·er
shale	ship·load
shal·low	ship·ment
sham	ship·wreck
shame	ship·yard
sham·poo	shirt
shape	shiv·er
share	shock
share·hold·er	shod
shark	shod·dy
sharp	shoe
sharp·en	shoe·lace
shat·ter	shoe·string
shave	shoot
shawl	shop
shear	shop·keep·er
sheath	shop·lift·er
sheaves	shore
shed	shorn

slop	snore
slope	snor·kel
sloth	snort
slouch	snout
slow	snow
sludge	snow·ball
slug	snow·drift
slug·gish	snow·fall
slum·ber	snow·flake
slump	snow·man
sly	snow·plow
smack	snow·storm
small	snub
smart	snuff
smash	snug
smear	snug·gle
smell	soak
smelt·er	soap
smile	soar
smirk	so·ber
smite	soc·cer
smit·ten	so·cia·ble
smock	so·cial
smog	so·cial·ist
smoke	so·ci·e·ty
smok·er	so·ci·ol·o·gy
smoke·stack	sock
smol·der	sock·et
smooth	so·da
smoth·er	so·di·um
smudge	so·fa
smug	soft
smug·gle	soft·ball
snag	soft·en
snail	sog·gy
snake	soil
snap	sol·ace
snare	so·lar
snarl	sold
snatch	sol·der
sneak	sol·dier
sneer	sole
sneeze	sol·emn
sniff	so·lem·ni·ty

so·lic·it	sound·proof
so·lic·i·tor	soup
sol·id	sour
sol·i·dar·i·ty	source
so·lid·i·fy	south
sol·i·tar·y	south·east
sol·i·tude	south·ern
so·lo	south·ward
sol·u·ble	sou·ve·nir
so·lu·tion	sov·er·eign·ty
solve	so·vi·et
sol·vent	sow
som·ber	soy·bean
some·bod·y	space
some·how	spa·cious
some·one	spade
some·place	spa·ghet·ti
some·thing	span
some·time	span·gle
some·what	span·iel
some·where	spank
son	spare
so·nar	spark
so·na·ta	spar·kle
song	spar·row
son·ic	sparse
son·net	spasm
soot	spas·mod·ic
soothe	spas·tic
so·phis·ti·cat·ed	spat
so·phis·ti·ca·tion	spa·tial
soph·o·more	spawn
so·po·rif·ic	speak
so·pran·o	speak·er
sor·cer·er	spear
sor·cer·y	spe·cial
sor·did	spe·cial·ist
sore	spe·cial·ize
sor·row	spe·cial·ty
sor·ry	spe·cies
sort	spe·cif·ic
sought	spec·i·fi·ca·tion
soul	spec·i·fy
sound	spec·i·men

speck	spoke
speck·le	spo·ken
spec·ta·cle	sponge
spec·tac·u·lar	spon·sor
spec·ta·tor	spon·ta·ne·ous
spec·ter	spool
spec·trum	spoon
spec·u·late	spo·rad·ic
spec·u·la·tion	sport
sped	spot
speech	spouse
speed	spout
speed·om·e·ter	sprain
speed·y	sprawl
spell	spray
spend	spread
spent	sprig
sphere	spright·ly
spher·i·cal	spring
spice	sprin·kle
spic·y	sprint
spi·der	sprout
spike	spruce
spill	sprung
spin	spry
spin·ach	spun
spi·nal	spur
spin·dle	spu·ri·ous
spine	spurn
spi·ral	sput·ter
spire	spy
spir·it	squad
spir·i·tu·al	squal·id
spit	squan·der
spite	square
splash	squash
splash·down	squat
spleen	squaw
splen·did	squeak
splen·dor	squeeze
splice	squire
splin·ter	squirm
split	squir·rel
spoil	squirt

stab
sta·bil·i·ty
sta·ble
stack
staff
stag
stage
stag·ger
stag·nant
staid
stain
stair
stair·case
stair·way
stake
stale
stale·mate
stalk
stall
stam·mer
stamp
stam·pede
stand
stand·ard
stand·ard·ize
stand-by
stand·point
stan·za
sta·ple
star
starch
stare
stark
star·ry
start
star·tle
star·va·tion
starve
state
state·ly
state·ment
states·man
states·man·ship
stat·ic

sta·tion
sta·tion·ar·y
sta·tion·er·y
sta·tis·tic
sta·tis·ti·cal·ly
stat·is·ti·cian
stat·ue
stat·ure
sta·tus
stat·ute
staunch
stay
stead·fast
stead·i·ly
stead·y
steak
steal
stealth
stealth·y
steam
steam·er
steam·ship
steel
steel·work·er
steep
stee·ple
steer
stem
stench
sten·cil
ste·nog·ra·pher
step
step·fa·ther
step·moth·er
ster·e·o
ster·e·o·phon·ic
ster·e·o·type
ster·ile
ster·i·lize
ster·ling
stern
stew
stew·ard
stick

stiff	straight·a·way
stiff·en	straight·en
sti·fle	straight·for·ward
stig·ma	strain
still	strain·er
stilt·ed	strait
stim·u·late	strand
stim·u·lus	strange
sting	stran·ger
stink	stran·gle
sti·pend	strap
stip·u·la·tion	stra·te·gic
stir	strat·e·gy
stir·rup	straw
stitch	straw·ber·ry
stock	stray
stock·bro·ker	streak
stock·hold·er	stream
stock·ing	street
stock·pile	strength
stock·room	stren·u·ous
sto·ic	stress
stole	stretch
sto·len	strew
stom·ach	strewn
stone	strick·en
ston·y	strict
stood	stric·ture
stool	stride
stoop	stri·dent
stop	strife
stop·o·ver	strike
stop·watch	string
stor·age	strin·gent
store	strip
store·house	stripe
store·room	strive
stork	strode
storm	stroke
sto·ry	stroll
stout	strong
stove	strong·hold
strad·dle	strove
straight	struck

struc·tur·al
struc·ture
strug·gle
strung
strut
stub·ble
stub·born
stuc·co
stuck
stud
stu·dent
stud·ied
stu·di·o
stu·di·ous
stud·y
stuff
stum·ble
stump
stung
stunt
stu·pe·fy
stu·pen·dous
stu·pid
stu·pid·i·ty
stu·por
stur·dy
sty
style
styl·ish
styl·ize
sub·con·scious
sub·di·vide
sub·due
sub·ject
sub·jec·tion
sub·ju·gate
sub·let
sub·li·ma·tion
sub·lime
sub·merge
sub·mis·sion
sub·mis·sive
sub·mit
sub·or·di·nate

sub·poe·na
sub·scribe
sub·scrip·tion
sub·se·quent
sub·ser·vi·ent
sub·side
sub·sid·i·ar·y
sub·si·dize
sub·sist
sub·sist·ence
sub·stance
sub·stan·tial
sub·stan·ti·ate
sub·sti·tute
sub·sti·tu·tion
sub·tle
sub·tract
sub·urb
sub·ur·ban
sub·ver·sive
sub·vert
sub·way
suc·ceed
suc·cess
suc·cess·ful
suc·ces·sion
suc·ces·sive
suc·ces·sor
suc·cinct
suc·cumb
suck
suck·le
suc·tion
sud·den
sue
suf·fer
suf·fice
suf·fi·cien·cy
suf·fi·cient
suf·fo·cate
suf·frage
sug·ar
sug·gest
sug·ges·tion

su·i·cide
suit
suit·a·ble
suite
suit·or
sul·fur
sulk·y
sul·len
sul·ly
sul·try
sum·ma·rize
sum·ma·ry
sum·ma·tion
sum·mer
sum·mit
sum·mon
sump·tu·ous
sun·beam
sun·burn
sun·down
sun·dry
sun·flow·er
sung
sun·glass·es
sunk
sun·light
sun·ny
sun·rise
sun·set
sun·shine
sun·spot
sun·tan
su·per·a·bun·dant
su·perb
su·per·fi·cial
su·per·flu·ous
su·per·high·way
su·per·in·tend·ent
su·pe·ri·or
su·pe·ri·or·i·ty
su·per·la·tive
su·per·mar·ket
su·per·nat·u·ral
su·per·sede

su·per·son·ic
su·per·sti·tion
su·per·struc·ture
su·per·vi·sion
su·per·vi·sor
sup·per
sup·plant
sup·ple
sup·ple·ment
sup·ple·men·ta·ry
sup·pli·ca·tion
sup·pli·er
sup·ply
sup·port
sup·pose
sup·po·si·tion
sup·press
su·prem·a·cy
su·preme
sur·charge
sure
sure·ty
surf
sur·face
surge
sur·geon
sur·ger·y
sur·ly
sur·mount
sur·name
sur·pass
sur·plus
sur·prise
sur·ren·der
sur·round
sur·veil·lance
sur·vey
sur·vey·or
sur·viv·al
sur·vive
sur·vi·vor
sus·cep·ti·ble
sus·pect
sus·pend

sus·pense
sus·pen·sion
sus·pi·cion
sus·pi·cious
sus·tain
su·ture
swal·low
swam
swamp
swan
swarm
swarth·y
sway
swear
sweat
sweat·er
sweep
sweep·er
sweet
sweet·en
sweet·heart
swell
swept
swerve
swift
swim
swim·mer
swin·dle
swine
swing
swirl
switch
swiv·el
swol·len
swoop
sword
sworn
swung
syl·la·ble
sym·bol
sym·bol·ize
sym·met·ri·cal
sym·me·try
sym·pa·thet·ic

sym·pa·thize
sym·pa·thy
sym·phon·ic
sym·pho·ny
sym·po·si·um
symp·tom
syn·a·gogue
syn·chro·nize
syn·di·cate
syn·o·nym
syn·op·sis
syn·the·sis
syn·thet·ic
sy·ringe
syr·up
sys·tem

T

tab·er·nac·le
ta·ble
ta·ble·cloth
ta·ble·spoon
ta·ble·spoon·ful
tab·let
ta·ble·ware
tab·loid
ta·boo
tab·u·lar
tab·u·late
tac·it
tack
tack·le
tact
tac·ti·cal
tac·tics
taf·fe·ta
tail
tail·gate
tai·lor
taint
take-off
take-o·ver
tale

tal·ent
talk
tall
tal·ly
tame
tan·gent
tan·gi·ble
tan·gle
tank
tan·ta·lize
tape
ta·per
tap·es·try
tar
tar·dy
tare
tar·get
tar·iff
tar·nish
tar·ry
tart
tar·tan
tar·tar
task
tas·sel
taste
tat·ter
tat·too
taught
taunt
tav·ern
taw·ny
tax
tax·a·tion
tax·i
tax·i·cab
tax·pay·er
tea
teach
teach·er
team
team·ster
team·work
tea·pot

tear
tease
tea·spoon
tech·ni·cal
tech·nique
tech·nol·o·gy
te·di·ous
tee
teem
teen-age
teeth
tel·e·cast
tel·e·gram
tel·e·graph
tel·e·phone
tel·e·scope
tel·e·type
tel·e·vise
tel·e·vi·sion
tell·er
tem·per
tem·per·a·ment
tem·per·ate
tem·per·a·ture
tem·pest
tem·ple
tem·po·rar·y
tempt
temp·ta·tion
te·na·cious
ten·ant
tend
ten·den·cy
ten·der
ten·don
ten·e·ment
ten·fold
ten·nis
ten·or
tense
ten·sion
tent
ten·ta·cle
ten·ta·tive

tenth
ten·u·ous
ten·ure
term
ter·mi·nal
ter·mi·nate
ter·mi·nol·o·gy
ter·race
ter·rain
ter·res·tri·al
ter·ri·ble
ter·ri·er
ter·rif·ic
ter·ri·fy
ter·ri·to·ri·al
ter·ri·to·ry
ter·ror
ter·ror·ism
ter·ror·ist
ter·ror·ize
test
tes·ta·ment
tes·ti·fy
tes·ti·mo·ny
text
text·book
tex·tile
tex·ture
than
thank
thank·ful
thanks·giv·ing
thatch
thaw
the·a·ter
the·at·ri·cal
theft
their
theme
them·selves
then
the·o·lo·gian
the·ol·o·gy
the·o·ret·i·cal

the·or·y
ther·a·pist
ther·a·py
there
there·af·ter
there·by
there·for
there·fore
there·up·on
there·with
ther·mom·e·ter
ther·mo·nu·cle·ar
ther·mo·stat
these
thick
thief
thieves
thigh
thin
thing
think
third
thirst
thirst·y
thir·teen
thir·ti·eth
thir·ty
tho·rax
thorn
thor·ough
thor·ough·fare
though
thought
thou·sand
thrall
thrash
thread
threat
three
thresh
thresh·old
threw
thrift
thrift·y

thrill	tin·der
thrive	tinge
throat	tin·gle
throb	tink·er
throm·bo·sis	tin·kle
throne	tin·sel
throng	tint
throt·tle	ti·ny
through	tip·toe
through·out	tire
throw	tire·some
thrust	tis·sue
thru·way	tithe
thumb	tit·il·late
thumb·nail	ti·tle
thumb·tack	tit·u·lar
thump	to
thun·der	toad
thun·der·bolt	toad·stool
thun·der·ous	toast
thun·der·storm	to·bac·co
thus	to·bog·gan
thwart	to·day
thy·roid	toe
tick	to·geth·er
tick·et	toil
tick·le	toi·let
tide	to·ken
ti·dings	told
ti·dy	tol·er·a·ble
tie	tol·er·ance
ti·ger	tol·er·ant
tight	tol·e·rate
tight·rope	toll
tile	to·ma·to
till	tomb
tilt	tomb·stone
tim·ber	to·mor·row
time	ton
time·ly	tone
tim·er	tongs
time·ta·ble	tongue
tim·id	ton·ic
tinc·ture	to·night

ton·nage
ton·sil
too
took
tool
toot
tooth
tooth·ache
tooth·brush
tooth·paste
top-heav·y
top·ic
top·i·cal
top-notch
to·pog·ra·phy
top·ple
torch
tore
tor·ment
torn
tor·na·do
tor·pe·do
tor·pid
torque
tor·rent
tor·sion
tor·toise
tor·tu·ous
tor·ture
toss
to·tal
to·tal·i·tar·i·an
tot·ter
touch
touch·down
tough
tour
tour·ist
tour·na·ment
tour·ni·quet
tow
to·ward
tow·el
tow·er

town
town·ship
towns·peo·ple
tox·ic
tox·ic·i·ty
tox·in
toy
trace
trac·er
track
tract
trac·ta·ble
trac·tion
trac·tor
trade-in
trade·mark
trad·er
tra·di·tion
traf·fic
trag·e·dy
trag·ic
trail
train
trait
trai·tor
tra·jec·to·ry
tramp
tram·ple
trance
tran·quil
tran·quil·iz·er
tran·quil·li·ty
trans·ac·tion
trans·at·lan·tic
tran·scend·ent
tran·scribe
tran·script
trans·fer
trans·fer·a·ble
trans·form
trans·fu·sion
trans·gress
trans·gres·sion
tran·sient

tran·sis·tor
tran·si·tion
trans·late
trans·la·tion
trans·mis·sion
trans·mit
trans·mit·ter
trans·par·ent
trans·plant
trans·port
trans·pose
trap
trash
trau·ma
trau·mat·ic
trav·ail
trav·el
trav·el·er
trav·erse
trawl·er
tray
treach·er·ous
treach·er·y
tread
trea·son
treas·ure
treas·ur·er
treas·ur·y
treat
treat·ment
trea·ty
tre·ble
tree
trem·ble
tre·men·dous
trem·or
trench
trend
tres·pass
tri·al
tri·an·gle
tribe
tri·bu·nal
trib·u·tar·y

trib·ute
trick
trick·le
tri·dent
tried
tri·fle
trig·ger
trig·o·nom·e·try
trill
tril·lion
tril·o·gy
trim
trin·i·ty
trip
tri·ple
trip·li·cate
tri·umph
tri·um·phal
tri·um·phant
triv·i·al
troll
troop
tro·phy
trop·ic
trop·i·cal
trot
trou·ble
trou·ble·some
trou·sers
trout
tru·ant
truce
truck
truc·u·lent
trudge
true
tru·ly
trump
trum·pet
trun·dle
trunk
truss
trust
trus·tee

trust·wor·thy
trust·y
truth
try
T-shirt
tube
tu·ber·cu·lo·sis
tuck
tuft
tu·i·tion
tu·lip
tum·ble
tu·mor
tu·mult
tu·mul·tu·ous
tu·na fish
tune
tun·er
tung·sten
tu·nic
tun·nel
tur·ban
tur·bine
tur·bu·lent
turf
tur·key
tur·moil
turn
tur·nip
turn·out
turn·o·ver
turn·pike
tur·pen·tine
tur·ret
tur·tle
tu·tor
tweed
twelfth
twelve
twen·ti·eth
twen·ty
twice
twig
twi·light

twill
twin
twine
twin·kle
twist
twitch
twit·ter
two
two·fold
type
type·writ·er
ty·phoid fe·ver
typ·i·cal
typ·ist
ty·ran·ni·cal
tyr·an·ny
ty·rant

U

ug·ly
ul·cer
ul·te·ri·or
ul·ti·mate
ul·tra·vi·o·let
um·brel·la
um·pire
un·a·ble
un·ac·com·pa·nied
un·ac·cus·tomed
u·nan·i·mous
un·armed
un·a·void·a·ble
un·a·ware
un·bal·anced
un·bear·a·ble
un·be·com·ing
un·be·liev·a·ble
un·bleached
un·born
un·bound
un·break·a·ble
un·bro·ken
un·can·ny

un·cer·tain
un·cer·tain·ty
un·changed
un·checked
un·civ·i·lized
un·cle
un·clean
un·com·fort·a·ble
un·com·mon
un·com·mu·ni·ca·tive
un·con·quer·a·ble
un·con·scious
un·con·sti·tu·tion·al
un·con·trol·la·ble
un·con·ven·tion·al
un·couth
un·cov·er
un·daunt·ed
un·de·cid·ed
un·de·ni·a·ble
un·der·arm
un·der·cov·er
un·der·cur·rent
un·der·de·vel·oped
un·der·es·ti·mate
un·der·foot
un·der·go
un·der·grad·u·ate
un·der·ground
un·der·hand·ed
un·der·line
un·der·mine
un·der·neath
un·der·pants
un·der·priv·i·leged
un·der·sell
un·der·shirt
un·der·stand
un·der·stood
un·der·take
un·der·tone
un·der·wa·ter
un·der·wear
un·der·writ·er

un·de·sir·a·ble
un·dis·ci·plined
un·dis·put·ed
un·dis·turbed
un·do
un·done
un·doubt·ed·ly
un·dress
un·due
un·dy·ing
un·eas·y
un·em·ployed
un·e·qualed
un·e·quiv·o·cal
un·err·ing
un·e·ven
un·ex·pect·ed
un·fair
un·fa·vor·a·ble
un·feel·ing
un·fin·ished
un·fit
un·fold
un·for·get·ta·ble
un·for·tu·nate
un·found·ed
un·friend·ly
un·furn·ished
un·god·ly
un·gra·cious
un·grate·ful
un·guard·ed
un·hap·py
un·health·y
un·hinge
un·ho·ly
un·hurt
u·ni·fi·ca·tion
u·ni·fied
u·ni·form
u·ni·form·i·ty
u·ni·lat·er·al
un·in·jured
un·in·tel·li·gi·ble

117

un·in·ter·est·ed
un·ion
u·nique
u·ni·son
u·nit
u·nite
u·ni·ty
u·ni·ver·sal
u·ni·verse
u·ni·ver·si·ty
un·just
un·kempt
un·kind
un·known
un·law·ful
un·less
un·like·ly
un·load
un·lock
un·luck·y
un·mis·tak·a·ble
un·mit·i·gat·ed
un·moved
un·nat·u·ral
un·nec·es·sar·y
un·oc·cu·pied
un·paid
un·par·al·leled
un·pleas·ant
un·prec·e·dent·ed
un·pre·dict·a·ble
un·prof·it·a·ble
un·qual·i·fied
un·ques·tion·a·bly
un·rav·el
un·rea·son·a·ble
un·re·lent·ing
un·re·served
un·re·strained
un·ri·valed
un·rul·y
un·safe
un·scru·pu·lous
un·sea·son·a·ble

un·seen
un·self·ish
un·set·tled
un·shak·en
un·sight·ly
un·skilled
un·sound
un·speak·a·ble
un·sta·ble
un·stead·y
un·suc·cess·ful
un·suit·a·ble
un·sus·pect·ed
un·think·ing
un·ti·dy
un·til
un·time·ly
un·to
un·told
un·touched
un·tried
un·true
un·used
un·u·su·al
un·veil
un·war·y
un·wel·come
un·will·ing
un·wise
un·wor·thy
un·yield·ing
up·braid
up·date
up·hold
up·hol·ster·y
up·keep
up·land
up·lift
up·per
up·per·most
up·right
up·ris·ing
up·roar
up·root

up·stairs
up·ward
ur·ban
urge
ur·gent
urn
us·a·ble
us·age
use
use·ful
use·less
ush·er
u·su·al
u·sur·y
u·ten·sil
u·ter·us
u·til·i·ty
u·ti·lize
ut·most
ut·ter

V

va·can·cy
va·cant
va·cate
va·ca·tion
vac·ci·nate
vac·cine
vac·u·um
va·grant
vague
vain
vale
val·en·tine
val·et
val·iant
val·id
va·lid·i·ty
val·ley
val·or
val·u·a·ble
val·u·a·tion
val·ue

valve
van·dal·ism
va·nil·la
van·ish
van·i·ty
van·quish
van·tage
va·por
va·por·ize
var·i·a·ble
var·i·a·tion
var·i·e·gat·ed
va·ri·e·ty
var·i·ous
var·nish
var·y
vase
vas·sal
vast
vault
vaunt
veal
vec·tor
veer
veg·e·ta·ble
veg·e·ta·tion
ve·he·ment
ve·hi·cle
veil
vein
ve·loc·i·ty
vel·vet
ve·neer
ven·er·a·ble
ve·ne·re·al
venge·ance
ven·om
ven·om·ous
vent
ven·ti·late
ven·ti·la·tion
ven·ture
ve·rac·i·ty
verb

ver·bal

ver·ba·tim

ver·bi·age

ver·dict

verge

ver·i·fi·ca·tion

ver·i·fy

ver·nac·u·lar

ver·nal

ver·sa·tile

verse

ver·sion

ver·sus

ver·te·brate

ver·ti·cal

ver·y

ves·sel

vest

ves·tige

vet·er·an

vet·er·i·nar·i·an

ve·to

vex·a·tion

vi·a

vi·a·ble

vi·al

vi·brate

vi·bra·tion

vi·car·i·ous

vice

vi·cin·i·ty

vi·cious

vic·tim

vic·tor

vic·to·ri·ous

vic·to·ry

vid·e·o·tape

view

view·point

vig·i·lance

vig·i·lant

vig·or·ous

vile

vil·lage

vil·lag·er

vil·lain

vin·di·cate

vin·dic·tive

vine

vin·e·gar

vine·yard

vin·tage

vi·nyl

vi·o·la·tion

vi·o·lence

vi·o·lent

vi·o·let

vi·o·lin

vi·per

vir·gin

vi·ril·i·ty

vir·tu·al

vir·tue

vir·tu·ous

vir·u·lent

vi·rus

vi·sa

vise

vis·i·bil·i·ty

vis·i·ble

vi·sion

vi·sion·ar·y

vis·it

vis·i·tor

vi·sor

vis·u·al

vi·tal

vi·ta·min

vi·va·cious

viv·id

vo·cab·u·lar·y

vo·cal

vo·ca·tion·al

vo·cif·er·ous

voice

void

vol·a·tile

vol·ca·no

vol·ley
volt
vol·ume
vo·lu·mi·nous
vol·un·tar·y
vol·un·teer
vo·lup·tu·ous
vom·it
vote
vot·er
vouch
vouch·er
vow
vow·el
voy·age
vul·gar
vul·ner·a·ble
vul·ture

W

wade
wa·fer
waf·fle
wage
wa·ger
wag·on
wail
waist
wait
wait·er
waiv·er
wake
walk
wall
wal·let
wal·low
wall·pa·per
wal·nut
wan
wand
wan·der
wane
wan·ton

ward
ward·en
ward·robe
ware
ware·house
war·fare
war·head
warm
warmth
warm-up
warn
warp
war·path
war·rant
war·ran·ty
war·ri·or
war·ship
wart
war·time
war·y
wash
wash·cloth
wash·er
wash·room
wasp
waste
waste·bas·ket
waste·land
waste·pa·per
watch
watch·dog
watch·man
watch·word
wa·ter
wa·ter-col·or
wa·ter·fall
wa·ter·front
wa·ter line
wa·ter main
wa·ter·mel·on
wa·ter·proof
wa·ter·shed
wa·ter-ski
watt

wave	wept
wave·length	west
wa·ver	west·ern
wax pa·per	whale
way	wharf
way·lay	wharves
way·side	what·ev·er
way·ward	wheat
weak	wheel
weak·ling	wheel·chair
wealth	whelp
wean	whence
weap·on	when·ev·er
wear	where·as
wea·ri·ness	where·by
wea·ri·some	where·fore
wea·ry	where·up·on
wea·sel	wher·ev·er
weath·er	wheth·er
weath·er·proof	which·ev·er
weave	while
weav·er	whim
wed·ding	whim·si·cal
wedge	whim·sy
wed·lock	whine
weed	whip
week	whirl
week·day	whirl·pool
week·end	whirl·wind
weep	whisk
weigh	whis·per
weight	whis·tle
weird	whit
wel·come	white
weld	white-col·lar
wel·fare	whit·en
well-be·ing	white·wash
well-de·vel·oped	whiz
well-in·formed	who·ev·er
well-known	whole
well-pre·served	whole·heart·ed
well-to-do	whole·sale
welt	whole·some

whole-wheat	wis·dom
whol·ly	wise
whore	wise·crack
whose	wish
wick	wisp
wick·ed	witch
wide	witch·craft
wid·en	with·draw
wide·spread	with·drew
wid·ow	with·hold
width	with·in
wield	with·out
wife	with·stand
wig·gle	wit·ness
wild	wit·ty
wild·cat	wiz·ard
wil·der·ness	wob·ble
wild·fire	woe
will·ful	wolf
will·ing	wolves
wil·low	wom·an
wilt	womb
wil·y	wom·en
wince	won
wind	won·der
wind·fall	won·der·ful
wind·mill	wood
win·dow	wood·chuck
wind·pipe	wood·en
wind·shield	wood·land
wind-up	wood·man
wind·y	wood·peck·er
wine	wood·shed
wing	wood·wind
wing·spread	wood·work
wink	wood·y
win·ner	woof
win·now	wool
win·ter	wool·en
win·try	wool·ly
wipe	word
wire	wore
wire·tap·ping	work

work·book
work·day
work·er
work·man
work·out
work·shop
world
world·ly
world·wide
worm
worn
wor·ry
worse
wor·ship
worst
worth
wor·thi·ness
worth·less
worth·while
wor·thy
would
wound
wove
wo·ven
wran·gle
wrap
wrap·per
wrath
wreak
wreck
wren
wrench
·wrest
wres·tle
wretch·ed
wring
wrin·kle
wrist
writ
write
writ·er
write-up
writ·ten

wrong
wrong·do·er
wrote

X

X·ray (ray)

Y

yacht
yard
yard goods
yard·stick
yarn
yawn
year
year·book
yearn
yeast
yel·low
yelp
yeo·man
yes·ter·day
yield
yo·ga
yo·gurt
yoke
yolk
yon·der
young
young·ster
your
yours
youth
youth·ful
yo·yo

Z

zeal
zeal·ous
ze·bra

ze·nith
ze·ro
zest
zig·zag
zinc
Zip Code
zip·per

zir·con
zo·di·ac
zone
zo·o·log·i·cal
zo·ol·o·gy
zoom